A
Pilgrim in
Chinese
Culture

近
鄰

A Pilgrim in Chinese Culture

Negotiating Religious Diversity

J U D I T H A . B E R L I N G

Wipf & Stock
P U B L I S H E R S
Eugene, Oregon

Wipf and Stock Publishers
199 W 8th Ave, Suite 3
Eugene, OR 97401

A Pilgrim in Chinese Culture
Negotiating Religious Diversity
By Berling, Judith A.
Copyright©1997 Orbis Books
ISBN: 1-59752-235-X
Publication date 6/7/2005
Previously published by Orbis Books, 1997

This limited edition licensed by special permission of Orbis Books.

Contents

Prologue

In 1987 after twelve years of teaching Chinese religions in the Religious Studies department of Indiana University, I assumed the position of Dean and Vice President for Academic Affairs of the Graduate Theological Union (GTU).[1] This was more than a change of jobs; it was in several respects a fundamental move in my life.

The most obvious move was institutional—from a state university to a consortium of theological schools. The GTU (sometimes known informally as God Talk Unlimited) is comprised of nine theological schools (three Roman Catholic, one Episcopalian, one Unitarian-Universalist, four Protestant), with centers and institutes adding Jewish, Eastern Orthodox, and Buddhist voices, as well as those of Pacific and Asian Christians. The GTU is ecumenically structured, following the lines of religious diversity; each school or center is an autonomous institution which represents a particular voice or viewpoint. The GTU has a firm commitment to maintaining the independence and particular mission of each of the member institutions. The GTU is founded on the conviction that bringing diverse religious perspectives into dialogue in denominationally based curricula creates extraordinary theological education. In our daily life together we also come to know intimately the challenges of religious difference. Through our experience, we become adept at what I have termed "daily ecumenism," the sensitivities, mutual understanding, and skills required to negotiate religious difference as part of our common life.

The move to the GTU was also geographic, a shift from the Midwest to Northern California, from the Bible Belt to the Pacific Rim. Although every corner of U.S. culture is increasingly marked by cultural diversity, such diversity is particularly vibrant in Northern California. As many have noted, California's demography is a window on the American future, for the coming century will be increasingly dominated by Pacific economies and cultures. As Europe was once the world's center of gravity, in the next century we will increasingly look to Asia. As a scholar of Chinese religions, the promise of a Pacific century fascinates me—the implications for our culture are myriad. The diversity of Northern California is not simply cultural or ethnic; it is also religious. Its religious landscape goes far beyond Jews and Christians to include Hindus, Muslims, Sikhs, Buddhists, Afro-Brazilian cults, new age groups, Druids, and a host of others. Living in Northern California brings the issue of diversity—both cultural and religious—very close to home. Californians are beginning to realize the implications of the world into which we are moving.

The move was also a move from religious studies to theological education. The shift of context from university to theological school entailed a serious reconsideration of the focus of my teaching and writing. The theological world demanded that I locate myself and my commitments and that I address the religious issues vital to theological studies. My thirty-year pilgrimage in Chinese studies could no longer be cast as study *about* Chinese religions, as many in religious studies would have it[2]; I was now faced with the implications of the study of Chinese religions for my own faith and for other persons of faith. I was asked not only what I knew *about* China, but also what I as a person of faith had learned *from* China.

As a teacher I have always sought to bring Chinese religions alive for my students. My twelve years at Indiana University convinced me that teaching Asian religions was a fundamental contribution to helping Americans learn to live in a pluralistic world.[3] My move to theological education, however, challenged me to articulate the implications of my work for those studying and working within the context of religious communities.

It has taken me some time to find my *theological* voice as a scholar of Chinese religions. First, I had to be clear that I am not a spokesperson for Chinese religions. As deeply as I have been enriched by my encounters with Chinese religions on all levels, I am neither Chinese nor a follower of any Chinese tradition. I have gained much in the way of wisdom and spiritual insight from Chinese teachers, living and dead, to whom I defer for faithful interpretations of the spiritual core of their traditions. My role is to assist others to understand Chinese religions, serving as a cultural bridge by invoking the authoritative voices of Chinese masters and explaining the context in which they taught and practiced.[4] My community and my audience is that of North American Christians; I want to help them to understand and appreciate the spiritual practices of the Chinese with "joy and equality."[5]

Second, as one who has learned the languages, struggled with the texts, and considered the complexities of Chinese history, I aim to provide textured accounts of how practices, ideas, or institutions functioned in their cultural settings. Ideas or practices lifted from a cultural setting may seem more accessible, but they can seriously mislead and compound misunderstandings. Although I want to help theological colleagues learn *from* and not just *about* Chinese religions, I am aware of the dangers of not attending carefully to the distinctively Chinese. One must look and listen carefully, seeking to understand the Chinese as much as possible on their own terms, before jumping to the stage of drawing lessons for oneself. Learning from another cultural and religious tradition requires respect and a willingness to stretch the horizons of understanding, to seek to imagine how their world and their faith looks to them.

Not wanting to speak for the Chinese but wanting to honor the rich cultural context, I have chosen in this book, and in my teaching and writing generally, to rely heavily on stories, both historical and based on personal experience. Stories have the advantage of creating a narrative world, a context.[6] A tale, like a biography, "forms a kind of looking-glass which enables readers to peer into—and step through into—another world."[7]

My tales are deliberately chosen to represent different times and places, to offer a range of perspectives on the diversity and richness of traditional Chinese religious practices. They include tales of my own experience (in which I am both a participant and the narrator) and tales told from the viewpoint of some particular person, event, or period in Chinese history. The book is structured thematically rather than historically, suggesting the development of my insights into Chinese religious life, as I have reconstructed them ex post facto. I have deliberately juxtaposed figures and events from different historical settings when they seem to speak to a common theme. On the other hand, tales are told with some attempt to convey their location and specificity. I do not attempt an encompassing narrative which would convey "Chinese religions" or the relationship of Chinese religiosity and Christianity.[8] The tales are intentionally fragmentary and specific, glimpses into another religious world, but not a comprehensive portrait.

My use of stories is, at least implicitly, a dialogical method for imparting information—a story assumes an audience. It invites the audience into the narrative world, inviting them to imaginatively "try on" an aspect of Chinese culture, and empowering them as observers and interpreters of that world. Through the use of stories I seek both to engage the readers' interest and also to invite them to draw their own interpretations, particularly as to how the Chinese stories might relate to their own lives.

The development of these stories and this manuscript has also been dialogical in practice; without the aid of valued colleagues, who kindly acted as my audience and my critics, this book would never have been written.

My primary dialogue partner has been Margaret McLean, who has worked with me as a Newhall fellow[9] for five years, developing this and other manuscripts. Margaret is a specialist in health care ethics, not a scholar of Chinese studies. That choice was intentional, since the audience for this book was to be outside of the Chinese field. Margaret has pushed me to identify and address my new audience. She has been an extraordinary critic and collaborator, muse and drill sergeant (keeping me on track and marching to cadence). Margaret's role in this project has been central; she is a full partner.

Jim Emerson, a friend and colleague from the GTU Board of Trustees, offered thoughtful comments on an early draft. Kevin Cheng, a GTU doctoral student from Hong Kong, served as a research assistant on an early draft, tracking down additional references and sources.

Thanks to Kevin Koczela for producing the models of the Chinese religious field in chapter 2.

In January 1994, Margaret and I took the manuscript formally to an "audience" by convening a Round Table of GTU faculty and doctoral students: Michael Aune, Dwight Hopkins, Mary Beth Lamb, Kenan Osborne, Kathryn Poethig, and Susan Smith. These stalwart colleagues discussed the manuscript for an entire day, offering extraordinary insights and encouragement for the work. Their comments sharpened the focus of this book.

During the fall semester of 1995, as the Ann Potter Wilson Distinguished Visiting Professor at the Divinity School at Vanderbilt University, I offered a doctoral seminar on the book manuscript. Six outstanding students—Emily Askew, Judith Bishop, Laurel Cassidy, Melissa Stewart, Minette Watkins, and Zhao Zuo—took this course, offering lively and insightful reactions to the manuscript.

In the spring semester of 1996, the manuscript was one of the texts for a reading course on Chinese religious practice taken by Geoff Foy and Denis Thalson at GTU. Their comments and responses were also immensely helpful.

I have shaped the stories to the responses of these audiences throughout the text and have sought to include their voices, particularly in the last chapter of reflections, in order to help to open up the tales to the readers' thoughts and interpretations.

The book is a collection of tales brought back from China by a pilgrim whose life has been profoundly enriched by her journey. Some of the tales are direct reports of my adventures in Taiwan; others are adventures I had in texts or in the course of study. All pertain, directly or indirectly, to the issue of living with religious diversity. They recount the examples which helped me appreciate Chinese strategies for living with religious neighbors, beginning from a premise of religious inclusivity (many Ways are valid) rather than exclusivity (there is only one true faith).

The book is organized in three sections. The first introduces the origins of my engagement with the issue of religious diversity and inclusivity, the shape of my pilgrimage in China, and my particular stance as an author. Chapter 1 introduces the concept of religious diversity and why it has become a central issue for me. Chapter 2 introduces my pilgrimage and how its meaning is shaped by Chinese notions of religious journey. Chapter 3 identifies my particular interpretive stance and distinguishes it from that of others who have sought to include interfaith views within Christian ecumenism.

The second section contains key tales from Chinese culture. Chapter 4 offers the notion of "religious field" as a way of modeling the dynamics of religious pluralism in Chinese culture. Chapter 5 explores the tensions between government and local communities over who governs the rules of play on the Chinese religious field. Chapter 6 speaks of how the myriad gods and deities in China are related to a transcendent spiritual unity. Chapter 7 discusses the distinctive Chinese notion of Truth as having many different embodiments. Chapter 8 discusses the patterns of hospitality which sustain a fragile balance of diverse religious communities in Chinese life.

The third section (chapter 9) invites readers to join in some reflections, to consider what insights the Chinese tales may offer us about living with religious diversity. This section begins the process of opening the stories from China to a range of reactions and interpretations from the cultural standpoint of North American Christians, seeing whether the alternative model presented by China does indeed help us to see with fresh eyes new possibilities for our own traditions.

Explanations for the Chinese characters that accompany each chapter appear at the foot of the first page of the chapter.

Time Line

Note on Chinese Romanization: This book uses the Wade-Giles system of Romanization of Chinese rather than the Pinyin system currently used in newspapers and periodicals because the bulk of research on traditional Chinese religions is still in Wade-Giles.

Shang Dynasty
c. 1523-1122 B.C.E.

System of priest-kings preserved on oracle bones

Chou Dynasty
1122-256 B.C.E.
(Warring States)
(403-221 B.C.E.**)**

Confucius, 551-479 B.C.E.
Mencius, 372?-289? B.C.E.
Chuang Tzu, 369?-286? B.C.E.
Lao Tzu, Sixth century, or Third century B.C.E.

Ch'in Dynasty
221-209 B.C.E.

Burning of the books

Former and Later Han
206 B.C.E. **- 8** C.E.
23-202 C.E.

Han historians, First century B.C.E.;
First century C.E.
Tung Chung-shu, 179?-104? B.C.E.
Chang Tao-ling, Second century C.E.

Period of Disunity
202-589 C.E.

Hsü Sun, 239-292
Monk Hui-yüan, 334-417
Neo-Taoists

Sui Dynasty
589-618

Emperor Yang-ti, r. 605-616

T'ang Dynasty
618-907

Monk Yüan-chien
Monk Hsüan-tsang (Tripitika), ca. 596-664

Veneration of Hsü Sun
Han Yü, 786-824
Monk Ennin, 798-864
Edict on Persecution of Buddhism,
845

Sung Dynasty
960-1279

Emperor Chen-tsung, r. 998-1022
Su Shih, 1037-1101
Liu Yi-chih, 1078-1160
Emperor Hui-tsung, r. 1102-1125
Chu Hsi, 1130-1200
Pai Yü-ch'an, 1194-1229
Li Ch'en, 1144-1218
Ch'iao Li-hsien, 1155-1222
Ch'en Nan (Ni-wan), 1171?-1213

Chin (Jurchen) Dynasty
1115-1234

Yüan (Mongol) Dynasty
1260-1368

Ming Dynasty
1368-1644

Emperor Ming T'ai-tsu, r. 1368-1398
Wang Yang-ming, 1472-1529
Wu Ch'eng-en, c. 1500-1582
Lin Chao-en, 1517-1598
Cho Wan-ch'un, Sixteenth century
Li Chih, 1527-1602
White Lotus movements strong

Ch'ing (Manchu) Dynasty
1644-1912

Republican Period
1912-1949

People's Republic of China
1949-present

A
Pilgrim in
Chinese
Culture

PART 1

Religious Diversity and the Pilgrimage to China

CHAPTER 1

Living with Religious Neighbors

Negotiating Religious Diversity

> But the lawyer, desiring to justify himself, said to Jesus, "And who is my neighbor?"
>
> *(Luke 10:29)*

Over the past few years I have heard three stories which touched a deep vein of hope all too often obscured by the contention of the 1990s.

Catholics and Buddhists

A Portuguese Catholic friend told me of a special Portuguese saints' day at a Bay Area parish during which the faithful deck the saints in flowers and carry them in the procession through the neighborhoods around the church. Vietnamese Buddhists who had settled in the community saw this festival, and it reminded them of their Buddhist festivals wherein they deck the Buddha-images with flowers and parade them through the neighborhood. Seeing a familiar religious practice, the Buddhists joined in the Catholic festival, and an interfaith friendship was begun.

"Close Neighbor"
Literally, nearby village, and by extension, neighbors. The term would include those with whom one had regular encounters (at markets, etc.), but were the members of one's own clan.

近
鄰

Tlingits and Russian Orthodox

> On a visit to Sitka, Alaska, I learned that when the Russian settlers married into native Tlingit clans, they devised an ingenious way to honor both native and Russian Orthodox traditions for funerals: the funeral would begin in the Tlingit long-house with traditional ceremonies and then would solemnly process to the Orthodox church for a funeral. A shared tradition of funerary processions helped to tie together the long-house ceremonies and the Orthodox funeral.

Evangelical Christians and the Chinese Moon Festival

> After a lecture I gave at Western Illinois University, an evangelical Christian shared with me that their church had opened a center for international students, including students from China. In order to make the Chinese students feel more welcome, she told me, the church had invited the Chinese to celebrate their Moon Festival with the members of the local congregation.

These three stories represent relatively rare successes at bridging religious boundaries, opening communities in our increasingly diverse society to the richness of living with religious neighbors. The troubling question is, why are such stories so rare?

One answer is that the scope of religious diversity in our society has expanded. Where U.S. society could once be appropriately analyzed in terms of *Protestant, Catholic, Jew,*[1] such a depiction would now not only be simplistic, it would be downright inaccurate. As Diana Eck has noted, "By the 1990s, there were Hindus, Sikhs, Buddhists, and Jains. There were more Muslims than Episcopalians, more Muslims than Presbyterians, perhaps soon more Muslims than Jews." In her Harvard classes in the 1990s, she was struck that the representatives of "Asian" religions were now American citizens. "There were Muslims from Providence, Hindus from Baltimore, Sikhs from Chicago, Jains from New Jersey. They represented the emergence in America of a new cultural and religious reality."[2] Our communities, our schools, our workplaces, our hospitals, and even our families are increasingly inter-religious.[3] Moreover, as Eck's article points out, we can no longer neatly relegate those "other religions" to other parts of the world.

> Today, the Islamic world is no longer somewhere else, in some other part of the world; instead, Chicago with its 50 mosques and nearly half a million Muslims is part of the Islamic world.

[handwritten margin note, left side, rotated: "Doesn't that seem obvious? Isn't that what America is about?"]

America today is part of the Islamic, the Hindu, the Confucian world. It is precisely the interpenetration of ancient civilizations and cultures that is the hallmark of the late twentieth century. *This* is our new georeligious reality. The map of the world in which we now live cannot be color-coded as to its Christian, Muslim, or Hindu identity, but each part of the world is marbled with the colors and textures of the whole.[4]

More clearly than ever before in history, these folks are indeed our religious neighbors, not only globally, but also locally. Yet Christians and Jews have developed few positive resources for understanding and developing positive relationships with religious neighbors; we still carry the weight of centuries (if not millennia) of exclusivistic attitudes and patterns of association.

One has only to open a daily newspaper to grasp that religious difference is a volatile—even a deadly—force in our contemporary world: in Rwanda, Bosnia-Herzegovina, the former Soviet Union, the Arab states, and Israel. In the United States, tensions between Native American religious groups and the courts, between African-Americans and Jews, and between pro-life and pro-choice forces all have religious undercurrents. Too often we see religion as a force which divides us into hostile camps. The response is either to pull back into our own community and raise the fences higher, or to leave religion behind altogether. Neither strategy will help us to negotiate religious diversity. We need to find some ground of mutual respect and genuine conversation with neighbors from many traditions and cultural backgrounds, a ground from which we can join in the effort to face the deep ethical and spiritual issues confronting humankind.[5]

In his book *Race Matters*, Cornel West has commented on the racial and religious strains between American blacks and Jews:

> The present impasse in black-Jewish relations will be overcome only when self-critical exchanges take place within and across black and Jewish communities not simply about their own group interest but also, and, more importantly, about what being black or Jewish means in *ethical terms*. This kind of reflection should not be so naive as to ignore group interest, but it should take us to a higher moral ground where serious discussions about democracy and justice determine how we define ourselves and our politics and help us formulate strategies and tactics to sidestep the traps of tribalism and chauvinism.[6]

West argues that the ethical identity of blacks is rooted in religion and music. He writes: "The best of black culture, as manifested, for example, in jazz or the prophetic black church, refuses to put whites or

近
鄰

Jews on a pedestal or in the gutter" (114). West's book is important for many reasons, but one of them is that he articulates the moral, religious, and cultural dimensions of tensions too often dismissed as merely racial or political. Moreover, he notes that religion can be a key part of the solution, and not simply a part of the problem. Religion contains the best of our cultures, even if we do not always act upon the best in our religions.

We must learn to live with religious difference, or else the fabric of our society will be rent asunder; the rich tapestry of U.S. culture will fray into a mass of tangled threads. This is an issue about which I care, worry, and pray, and to which I dedicate my work, including this book.

Several formative encounters with "difference" led me to the study of traditional Chinese religions, where I discovered a rich alternative model for understanding religious diversity.

Encounters with Difference and Discovery of China

When I was ten years old, my family moved from the northern Midwest to the boot heel of Missouri in the deep South. The year was 1955, the year of *Brown vs. the Board of Education*. At the turbulent beginning of the Civil Rights Movement, we were Yankees in the South. I was just old enough to experience this as a severe culture shock. If I ever had views of a single "American" culture, my experience in the South undermined them. I was deeply attracted to parts of Southern culture and profoundly confused by or resistant to others; but through it all, I knew I was a Yankee and did not belong.

After a year in Missouri, my family moved to Dubuque, Iowa. As Presbyterians in Roman Catholic Dubuque (75 percent Catholic and known as "little Rome"), we were members of a religious minority. In Dubuque, church and church-related activities mattered: pre-Vatican II Dubuque was still fighting the Reformation; everyone in town could identify Protestant and Catholic properties and businesses; and there were street fights between Catholic and Protestant youth.[7] If you were a Dubuque Protestant, you knew the doctrinal and liturgical reasons why. Church and church-related activities were the nexus of social as well as religious life, since the Protestant leaders wanted to keep the youth not only in the church, but in the right church! Accordingly, I was deeply involved in church activities, concerned to locate myself in this world of religious competition, so that I could maintain my heritage, which I, of course, was convinced was the right one.

Caught up in the ecumenical fervor surrounding Vatican II, I majored in religion at Carleton College in Northfield, Minnesota. For two years, I belonged to a student team ministry which served as the collective (unordained) pastor of a tiny United Church of Christ parish in

Zumbrota, Minnesota. I was headed for Union Theological Seminary in New York, and ordination. However, two experiences transformed my tidy world. First, one Sunday in 1966, I took a close college friend with me to the church in Zumbrota. My friend was Japanese. Takashi was an articulate, gentle Christian, and I was completely unprepared for how he would be received in Zumbrota.

I brought him to the church to meet the parishioners and to share something of his faith journey and his cultural background. The parishioners, however, were stiff and uncomfortable with him, and one began a question with, "Why do you Japs . . . ?" To my shock and chagrin, these good Christian folk unabashedly laid on him their angry stereotypes of Asians. Both he and I came away more than a little shaken. I had become increasingly aware of racism as a cancer in our society, but it had never shoved its face so forcefully into mine; this experience taught me profoundly about our culture's fear and ignorance of Asians.

Shortly thereafter, a course on Chinese religions dramatically opened up my world, putting me literally in awe of the depth and richness of this culture so little known and understood in the West. Here was an entire stream of cultural and spiritual heritage of which I had no inkling; my former vision of what it meant to be well learned and "cosmopolitan" was stretched until it burst like a bubble.[8] "Asia" was not absent from cultural parlance in the 1960s; at times it seemed that "Asia" was everywhere. There were at least three contending views of Asia in the U.S. culture of the 1960s, not one of them remotely accurate: not the stereotypes of Asians in the context of the Vietnam War; not the denunciations of experimentation with Eastern religions as "a loss of values"; and not the claims of pop culture to be "into" Eastern religions.

Perhaps because of my Dubuque experience, with its emphasis on religious identity and tradition as defining the boundaries of the "right" and "the normal," I became convinced that Americans needed a broader cultural and religious horizon in order to negotiate an increasingly diverse world. I was no longer comfortable in the worlds of Dubuque or Zumbrota. Because in Dubuque and Zumbrota, Asia was not really part of the world, it followed all too readily that Asians were not fully human, and Asian religions were construed either as exoticized rebellion or dangerous heresy. My experience of middle-America was that it was far from ready for what some now speak of as the "Pacific century," but even in the mid-1960s the Pacific was on the horizon, either as a promise or as a threat.

In that semester, in that course, my deepening sense of the injustice and ignorance of racism was dramatically juxtaposed to the broadening of my cultural and ethicospiritual horizons in the course on China. I had discovered a vocation, a significant lifetime undertaking. It be-

近
邻

came clear to me that through learning and teaching about China I could seek to perform a ministry which would work at eroding the foundations of racism and building the foundations of cross-cultural understanding.

As a junior, I dropped my plans for seminary and opted instead to study Chinese language, culture, and religion in a doctoral program at Columbia University in New York. I wanted to learn the language, immerse myself in the literature and history, live among the people, visit temples and experience the worship, in order to understand more fully the richness of the heritage; and then I wanted to interpret what I had learned for those who had not had such experiences first-hand. I sought to become a cultural bridge, one who could translate and interpret Chinese cultural values and beliefs in ways that would help others see their value and appreciate their contributions to the global heritage. In her writings Carter Heyward has linked the notion of a bridge to the ideal of transcendence. She writes, "To transcend means, literally, to cross over. To bridge. To make connections. To burst free of particular locations."[9] By becoming a bridge, I hoped to transcend and help others to transcend limited horizons, thereby advancing the cause of multicultural understanding, since mutual ignorance and suspicion seemed to be at the root of so much of the world's pain and injustice.

My sojourn into the depth and richness of Chinese culture did not uproot me from Western culture, but it put Western culture and its achievements into a fuller, more global context. It taught me at a deep level that the story of the West is not *the* font of human achievement, but is rather *one* story and source of human achievement. Seen in a global perspective, not only could the great achievements of Western culture be celebrated as *not inevitable*, and therefore remarkable, but also the failures or inadequacies of Western cultural history could be also seen as *not inevitable*, and therefore as examples of human fallibility from which humankind might learn.

China and Religious Diversity

My discovery of China was at first a simple but dramatic broadening of my cultural horizons, a call to a broader and more inclusive vision of the rich human heritage. However, as I experienced more of Chinese culture and religion, I began to understand my deeper attraction, what I sought in this foreign land. Traditional Chinese religion compelled my attention because of one striking characteristic: that while the Christian history of Europe and North America had been shaped by exclusivist and sectarian forces, the traditional history of Chinese religions had been based on the opposite, inclusivist, premise.

This premise was stated succinctly by the early student of Chinese religions, W. E. Soothill:

While a few of the laity devote themselves, some solely to Buddhism, some solely to Taoism, the great mass of the people have no prejudices and make no embarrassing distinctions; they belong to none of the three religions [Buddhism, Taoism, or Confucianism], or, more correctly, they belong to all three. In other words, they are eclectic, and use whichever form best responds to the requirement of the occasion for which they use religion.[10]

This striking contrast to the patterns of the monotheistic cults of Christianity and Judaism created a very different cultural dynamic of religious diversity. Traditional Chinese life entailed a rich pattern of religious diversity. As Valerie Hansen has written:

Temples dedicated to popular deities studded the medieval Chinese landscape. Contemporary writers pointed out that even the smallest villages contained more than one temple, while temples in the large cities numbered in the hundreds. The laity asked the gods to bring rain, to clear the skies, to drive out locusts, to expel bandits, to suppress uprisings, to cure illnesses, to enable them to conceive, to prevent epidemics, and to help them pass the civil service examinations.[11]

The diversity of religious groups and practices in every Chinese community constituted a rich religious field in which to pursue both worldly and other-worldly goals. Over the centuries, the Chinese developed strategies for living with religious diversity, and these strategies offer a suggestive alternative to the exclusivistic model for a religiously plural society, a hypothetical case that can help us to see new options and possibilities. The Chinese case invites us to ask a series of questions:

- What happens if a society starts from the premise of inclusivity, that religions are not mutually contradictory, and that multiple religious affiliation is not dangerous, but is perhaps the norm?
- What happens if religious organizations are hospitable to one another in order to create and sustain the larger community?
- What happens if a culture develops patterns to create and sustain mutual familiarity and regular interaction among members of various religious groups?

Traditional China does not hold all the answers to the challenge of religious diversity, but it provides a useful model for understanding what would be entailed in an inclusivist approach to religious difference.

This book shares what I have learned as a pilgrim in Chinese culture around the issues of religious diversity. Although my initial visit to East Asia was long ago, the pilgrimage has continued as I have pur-

近
邻

sued my studies. China is a rich and complex land with many faces; the stories of my pilgrimage and the tales of China will not all focus narrowly on diversity, but they will provide the context for understanding something of how and why the Chinese negotiated the religious differences in their culture. I hope that this book will open up horizons for those seeking to negotiate cultural and religious diversity more effectively.

The other two chapters in this section will help to situate this book and my stance as author. Chapter 2 will articulate how my nearly thirty years of study and travel have been a pilgrimage of self-discovery and broadening horizons. It will begin to identify the theological dimensions of the enterprise. Chapter 3 will locate my particular approach in this book among other approaches to interfaith understanding.

西
遊
記

The Pilgrimage and the Pilgrim

She who would valiant be 'gainst all disaster,
let her in constancy follow the Master.
There's no discouragement
shall make her once relent
her first avowed intent
to be a pilgrim.

Who so beset her round with dismal stories,
do but themselves confound, her strength the more is.
No foes shall stay her might,
though she with giants fight;
she will make good her right
to be a pilgrim.

Since, Lord, thou dost defend us with thy Spirit,
we know we at the end shall life inherit.
Then fancies flee away;
I'll fear not what they say,
I'll labor night and day
to be a pilgrim.

—*Percy Dearmer, after John Bunyan*
Hymn #564, Episcopal Hymnal
(adapted for female "pilgrim")

"Journey to the West"
Journey to the West is the name of a popular Chinese novel, about a famous pilgrim's search for Buddhist truth on a trip to India, to be discussed in this chapter.

西
遊
記

Pilgrimage to Lion's Head Mountain

In December 1971, I had been living in Taipei for three months, honing my spoken Chinese, studying calligraphy, visiting temples, observing traditional rituals, and collecting books on Chinese religion and culture. Just before Christmas, I asked my Taipei colleague Cynthia McLean to join me on a visit to Lion's Head Mountain (Shih T'ou Shan), a Buddhist pilgrimage site in central Taiwan. What started as a pleasant outing turned into an extraordinary adventure, a pilgrimage which provided a frame of meaning for my studies in Chinese culture.[1]

Taipei in the 1970s was brimming with traditional Chinese religious practices, but these were tucked into the corners and back alleys of a rapidly modernizing city. The journey to Shih T'ou Shan was, symbolically, a journey back to more traditional times. This was marked in part by our modes of transportation. We set out from Taipei on a rapid modern train, transferred to a nice bus, then transferred again to an old, rickety bus that carried almost as many chickens as people. The town at the base of Lion's Head Mountain still offered pedicabs as its primary mode of public transportation, and the town store (which catered mainly to pilgrims) lacked the amenities common to urban shops. The ladies room, for instance, was a privy adjacent to the pigsty, down a ladder below the shop, a clear signal that we were entering a different world.

As we left the town and started up the mountain, vestiges of the modern world faded, save for the watches and cameras of the pilgrims. The only paths were footpaths, and supplies were delivered by the traditional Chinese mode of slinging items from a long pole balanced across the shoulders. As the modern world receded, the world of traditional Buddhism and Chinese religions appeared before us. The mountain displayed a comprehensive vision of Chinese religious life, with multiple levels of faith, many streams of practice. As the pilgrims climbed, we advanced through layers of religious imagination, spiritual discipline, and symbolism. After devoting five years to the study of Chinese religions, I finally came to understand on this mountain that, for the Chinese, the many forms of religious expression were all aspects of a single Way.

At the first stop on the climb, easily accessible to all visitors, there were attractions for the children. Most striking, in 1971, was a tiny coin-operated carousel of flags of the United Nations,[2] and another carousel depicting the Eight Immortals of "Taoist" folk religion.[3] At this stop, grannies, aunts, or big sisters were left to mind the small children, while others continued up the path. But even at this "children's corner" the carousels taught basic principles of Chinese religion: patriotic virtue—in this case as Chinese citizens of the world

—and belief in spirits who can grant boons such as long life. They may not have come far, but all pilgrims who made it to this first stop had "entered the way," and would receive religious merit for their journey.

The subsequent gradual climb featured scenic views and eventually offered a vision of a temple ornately decorated with colored carved glass. The hips of the roof and every inch of eaves, pillars, and rafters pulsed with colorful carvings, statues, and paintings of popular Chinese folk deities. Closer inspection revealed walls covered with grisly scenes of sinners' torments in hell. Pilgrims could contemplate all this from comfortable benches while enjoying a snack blessed by a deity.

This temple displayed the basic premise of Chinese folk traditions: moral retribution for sins and reward for good deeds. The deities of the temple could assist the faithful in their struggle to defeat the powers of evil and ally themselves with the powers of good. The elaborate decorations caught the attention of the pilgrims, and the entire temple functioned as a text, a pedagogical tool. The illustrated myths and tales served as mnemonic or pedagogical devices for Chinese folk beliefs; even the illiterate (and they were legion in traditional China) could "read" this temple, provided they had at some time heard the tales from a family member or priest or seen them performed in a temple or village drama. They learned their religion by "reading" the text of temple paintings to reinforce what they had heard in story or drama. Such illustrated tales were the primary form of religious and moral education in traditional China.[4] Pilgrims at this temple imbibed the lessons of basic Chinese religious belief and were invited to make or renew a fundamental commitment to do good deeds. Thus they would seek the help of the gods to avoid the torments of hell so graphically depicted on the walls of this temple, and to win rebirth in heaven, as depicted on the main altars.

As we left this temple and ascended the steep path along increasingly dramatic mountain vistas, the crowd of pilgrims began to thin. Each new temple was less colorful and folksy; the number and density of illustrations waned; interiors grew dim; and deities represented higher ranks in the Buddhist pantheon. Taoist and folk deities had by and large disappeared. Gilt images of Buddhas and Bodhisattvas shone mysteriously in the dim light of rooms redolent of generations of incense. The long vistas and the silent temples drew pilgrims symbolically into the dual cultivation of Buddhist wisdom. Buddhist practice produces both insight or vision (*kuan*) and stillness or quiescence (*chih*). The sweeping scenic expanses on the way up the mountain symbolized the development of broader insight or vision, while the silent dimness of the temples evoked stillness. These well-placed mountain shrines offered a foretaste of the fruits of this religious path, in which adepts cultivate insight and quiescence through the discipline of meditation.

西
遊
記

After a rigorous climb to a spot near the peak of the mountain, the few remaining pilgrims reached an active monastery where pilgrims could stay, for a modest offering, as long as we observed the monastic schedule of the monks during the visit (bath, vegetarian meal, vespers, early bed, predawn worship, vegetarian breakfast). My friend and I gladly accepted the hospitality offered. During meals we had opportunity to chat with the monks and the abbot about Buddhist teachings and life. An overnight stay in the monastery gave us a taste of the monastic path: the order and ascetic simplicity of daily life; the monotonous vegetarian meals, which gradually weaned monks from the delights of the world; the quiet pleasures of regular worship; the steady focus on spiritual formation through every activity. The abbot was a delightful host who emanated great joy and peace. His warmth and gentle instruction made us wish for a longer visit, even though we were not sure that we could long sustain the rigors of monastic life.

I was thrilled when, as I made ready to depart, the abbot offered me a parting gift of Buddhist scriptures hand-copied by the monks. His gift not only honored my willingness to learn about his faith, but also made me a "real" Buddhist pilgrim. In historical times, the Chinese emperors commissioned famous monks (like Hsüan-tsang [c. 596-664], immortalized in the novel *Journey to the West*) to undertake pilgrimages to India to collect and bring back to China Buddhist scriptures. Later Japanese Buddhist monks such as Ennin (798-864) came to China seeking Buddhist scriptures to take to Japan. More than a thousand years later, this abbot offered me hand-copied Buddhist scriptures as a token of my pilgrimage, assimilating me into a long line of pilgrims who had sought truth in faraway Buddhist monasteries.

After we bid our reluctant farewells, Cynthia and I chose to descend the mountain by the back way, and so experienced yet another dimension of Buddhist life and practice. Although it looked equal on the pilgrim's map we had purchased in town, the back way was in fact longer and more arduous, dotted with lonely hermitages of monks who had withdrawn into solitude for a period of silent contemplation and prayer. Several hermits had carved stone or wooden images of Buddhas in the walls of their caves or huts to provide them with spiritual companionship. If the front mountain path represented the way of communal and organized Buddhism, the rear path represented the solitary quest for realization of the Buddhist Way.

The Buddhists, in their distinctive fashion, did not explain the different levels of practice and iconography depicted on the various paths and by-ways of the mountain.[5] Yet the lessons were not lost on us or other pilgrims. The visual contrasts created strikingly different atmospheres of Chinese folk religion, Taoist worship, and Buddhist piety, which combined to depict a religious path with many layers of symbolism and practice, all of which, however, advanced one on the Way.

The Buddhists on this mountain, like many other schools or centers of Chinese religion, had absorbed into their religious vision a version of the entire Chinese religious field; all paths, they suggested, help the faithful in their spiritual progress.

西
遊
記

This journey helped me understand Chinese religious life; such was the major purpose of my stay in Taiwan. Yet for many years after that visit to Lion's Head Mountain, my thoughts returned to the days on that mountain with a persistent question: What had been the meaning of my pilgrimage? Why did I take it? Why, in fact, had I undertaken the study of Chinese religions? The journey to Shih T'ou Shan brought home to me that I was in Chinese culture as a pilgrim. What was I seeking there? What did I hope to bring back?

To Be a Pilgrim

The story of how I came to study Chinese religions provides a context of meaning for my pilgrimage to Lion's Head Mountain and in Chinese culture. This pilgrimage was first and foremost an intellectual sojourn, the project of a historian of Chinese religions. I had devoted myself to the study of Chinese religions and cultures. After four years of language study and course work at Columbia, I went to East Asia to write my dissertation, but also to experience and observe first-hand everything I could of Chinese religious life and practice. I frequented temples, festivals, and rituals, knowing that first-hand observation of religion would flesh out the picture I had gleaned from formal study. This was particularly important, since my classes at Columbia had focused on Chinese thought and history, not on the practices of Chinese religious life.[6] In Taiwan I had wonderful opportunities to observe the living practice of Chinese religions, to put the ideas and texts into the context of actual human behavior.

The pilgrimage was also, in a somewhat larger sense, a broadening of my cultural horizons, an extension of my experience and vision of the richness of the human heritage. My nearly three years in Asia during the research and writing of my dissertation offered an opportunity to steep myself in the art, literature, food, social patterns, and religions of East Asia: Taiwan, Japan, Korea, and Hong Kong. The experience of living in Taiwan stretched me in many ways. After some difficult adjustments, I began to feel comfortable—almost at home—in many aspects of East Asian culture. The pilgrimage to Lion's Head Mountain was an important piece of opening myself to the horizons of Chinese culture; never before or after did I immerse myself so completely in a traditional Chinese context. There were, for example, no modern amenities nor any English speakers, except Cynthia and myself, on Lion's Head Mountain. For this period, at least, I entered

西
遊
記

fully into a traditional Chinese setting. Thus my assimilation into the traditional pattern of the Buddhist pilgrim through the gift of the scriptures from the abbot was a kind of seal of this crossing of boundaries. Accepted into the company of Chinese Buddhist pilgrims, even temporarily, I had tangible confirmation that my cultural horizons had expanded. My world had grown to encompass realities from long ago and across the great waters.[7]

But if my pilgrimage had yielded intellectual understanding and expansion of my cultural horizons, it also had deeper implications. As I learned about Chinese religions, I also came to understand the deeper implications of my wanderings, for the notions of journey, wandering, path, and pilgrimage are central to Chinese metaphors for the religious life.

Chinese Notions of Religious Life as Pilgrimage

The notions of pilgrimage and wandering are central to the Chinese image and practice of the religious life. In this section, I will discuss the Chinese concept of Tao (path, way, and hence journey) as a basic metaphor for all of religious life. Then I will discuss the image of "wandering" as the means by which a person's soul or spirit matures and grows spiritually. Finally, I will relate the extraordinary religious pilgrimages of two Chinese thinkers who wandered beyond the bounds of their known world in order to discover a deeper religious vision.

Tao as Path—A Basic Metaphor

No term comes closer to conveying the Chinese equivalent of "religion" than "Tao." Tao, at base, means a footpath. The written character combines the pictorial elements of a foot and a leader—"a 'head' topped with the two plumes that were used in ancient days to signify the rank of general"[8] (see figure 2.1). Thus, Tao is a footpath going in a

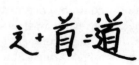

Figure 2.1

definite direction, or a path of action. From the notion of path or path of action, the character came to mean an art or skill, as in the Tao of archery. From this notion of art or skill, it further came to have connotations of the principles underlying the art or skill, hence a teaching, a way, an approach to either a specific arena of action or to life in general.

Very early in Chinese history, various religious groups used the term "Tao" as a label for the religious path, the practices and approach to life which their particular community advocated and lived. By extension, it stood for the truth or core of their teachings. Thus it was that the term came to be virtually synonymous with truth or source of truth; that which is and underlies all that is sacred and authentic.

西
遊
記

The concept of Tao is an important common term in Chinese religious life. Different teachers or communities had their own distinctive definitions of it. Some, like Lao Tzu (dates unclear; some say sixth century B.C.E.; others fourth or even third century B.C.E.), saw Tao as the ultimate, beyond which nothing existed.

> There is a thing confusedly formed,
> Born before heaven and earth.
> Silent and void
> It stands alone and does not change,
> Goes round and does not weary.
> It is capable of being the mother of the world.
> I know not its name
> So I style it "the way."[9]

For him, Tao was also the source of all that is, the origin of the cosmos. He wrote,

> The way begets one; one begets two; two begets three; three begets the myriad creatures.
> The myriad creatures carry on their backs the *yin* and embrace in their arms the *yang* and are the blending of the generative forces of the two. (XLII, p. 103)

For Buddhists or Confucians, Tao was the teachings, path, truth, or principles of Buddha or of the sages, an ultimate reality and approach to religious life expounded by the great masters. In all cases, however, Tao was the Way, the path of religious life with its appropriate teachings, principles, and arts.

The many layers of meaning of Tao—as path, as principle or truth, as skill or art—all shaped the Chinese image of religious life: as a path, as a way to be followed, as a pilgrimage. The pilgrims on Lion's Head Mountain were not simply performing a discrete act of travel to a sacred site. Because of the comprehensive vision of Chinese religious life on the mountain, they were also in effect retracing the whole of Chinese religious life. The outward journey to the mountain made visible the day-to-day sojourn of their own religious faith and practice.

The Chinese notion of religion as path, and of religious life as a pilgrimage through many layers and levels of spirituality, revealed to me the spiritual dimensions of the broadening of my cultural horizons. My pilgrimage in China was not only of body and intellect, but also of the soul or spirit. In Chinese religious life, the soul's progress came

西
遊
記

about through some form of "wandering"—either guided by ritual or meditative discipline or a roaming triggered by one's moral state and concerns.

Wanderings of the Spirit: Internal and "External"

In traditional China, there were rich traditions of travel of the soul (*shen*).[10] In many forms of Chinese ritual and meditation, the spirit of the practitioner might travel to the spirit world. In other rituals or meditations, a segment of the spirit world—for example a mandala or a set of deities—was introjected into the self.[11] In either case the distance between the practitioner's individual soul and the world of the spirits was bridged, causing the soul to make progress on its journey of realization of the Way. As the soul expanded in experience and command of the spirit world, it gained health and strength and perfected its skills and powers. Thus these travels of the soul were essential to the spiritual growth of the individual.

In some practices, the sojourn of the soul was charted step by step, as depicted in the symbolism and iconography of religious texts, art, and discourse. In Taoist Inner Alchemy (*nei-tan*) meditation, for instance, this internal pilgrimage led the spirit back to the very beginning of creation, when the Tao was unified and undifferentiated, before one begat two. Following the structures and symbols of the alchemical laboratory, various aspects of the physical vitality and spiritual-cognitive powers of the adept were gradually withdrawn from their dissipating entanglements with the external world of desires; quieted, cleansed, and purified; centered; and reunited to recover the original undifferentiated unity of Tao. This reunification was also a form of "intercourse," which "conceived" a new spiritual Self. The "spirit embryo" was carefully gestated and nurtured, until ready for its "birth" up channels along the spine and through the tiny anterior fontanelle, a hole at the top of the skull which is open at birth. This spiritual Self, at first weak and unstable like a new infant, learned gradually to wander, accumulating skills and strength, and to expand until it filled heaven and earth. When the spiritual Self was congruent with the universe, the practitioner had fully embodied the Way.[12]

The elaborate internal pilgrimage of Inner Alchemy Taoism was a complex process of meditative withdrawal, quiescence, reunification, rebirth, and the nurturing of a spiritual Self which had the capacity to embody the Tao completely. It was perhaps the most complex and fully developed of all of the techniques of Chinese meditation. The metaphor of pilgrimage was reinforced by the very gradualism and complexity of the process. It also covered vast—indeed cosmic—ground.

In popular culture, spirit travel functioned on two levels. First, Chinese popular religion offered a highly elaborated notion of the postmortem journey of the spirit through the courts of hell. Chinese rituals surrounding death attempted to call back the soul, which was believed to have departed the body. If the soul could be retrieved, the individual would recover from the death.[13] Once it was clear that the individual was irrevocably dead, the family sought through rituals, often accompanied by elaborate religious dramas, to provide various forms of assistance to the soul in its sojourn to the realms of the dead. These would include money to bribe officials and bridge keepers; horses, carriages, food, and servants[14]; spiritual escorts who knew the roads and could help the traveler negotiate pitfalls; spiritual merits of the living transferred or donated to the benefit of the deceased in order to balance off any outstanding sins; the intercession of deities, Buddhas, and Bodhisattvas who had clout with the judges of hell. Thus, in the minds of many Chinese, the longest and most dangerous religious journey was the posthumous search for a final resting place.

A second form of spirit travel in the popular imagination was the wandering of the soul or spirit during dreams. The Chinese understood dreams as the roaming of the spirit outside of the body. During these excursions the spirit could meet the souls of dead ancestors, run into ghosts or spirits, visit strange lands, and have a variety of adventures which could be terrifying or reassuring portents, or simply edifying experiences.

The Chinese soul traveled frequently, either in dreams or guided by meditation or ritual practice. The wanderings of the soul, guided or not, were paralleled by the spiritual-ethical journey of the individual in his or her lifetime. Those who followed the Way nurtured a healthy and strong spirit prepared for the afterlife. Those who did not would encounter difficulties and suffering in this life, or in the spirit world. The spiritual sojourn was not separate from the rest of the individual's life; it gave shape to all aspects of a person's life, now and in the hereafter. Likewise, the physical wanderings of persons in search of spiritual Truth nurtured the strength and powers of their soul.

Wanderers beyond the Bounds: Two Extraordinary Religious Journeys

The path of traditional Chinese religion incorporated the values and practices of Chinese religious life. Many people did not venture far along the path, sticking to a basic this-worldly religion of spiritual boons. There were those, however, whose experiences, gifts, and temperaments sent them on a long religious quest for a defining reality. They sought an authentic Way, a fresh vision of their distinctive place in the religious culture.

Such a one was Pai Yü-ch'an (1194-1229). The teachings he espoused, the rituals he practiced, and the traditions of the religious community whose history he recorded represented very different

西
遊
記

forms of Chinese religious life; yet in his pilgrimage, Pai was touched by them all.

When Pai Yü-ch'an's father died in his youth, he left home to follow the Taoist master Ch'en Nan (Ni-wan) (1171?-1213) for nine years and to learn from him the arts of Inner Alchemy meditation and Taoist thunder rites.[15] Pai's early life story suggests that the Taoistic[16] notion of living *fang-wai* (outside the bounds of normal society) sometimes—perhaps often—had real social roots; some Taoists left home, but others were left rootless by circumstances beyond their control. The cultural trope of the Taoist wandering beyond the bounds provided a mode by which to resolve an anomalous social status.

Pai became the formal disciple of Ch'en Nan in 1205. In 1213, when he realized the Way for himself (*te-tao*), he was formally initiated by Ch'en. From that time on, students and scholars from the four directions gathered around Pai Yü-ch'an "like the hairs on a bull."[17] Pai drew deeply from the common pool of Chinese religious practices and teachings, appropriating many ideas from them alongside those he had acquired from Ch'en Nan. He established a permanent retreat on Mt. Wu-i, on the border of Kiangsi and Fukien. There he gathered disciples and was visited by scholars and religious personalities; on his travels he met many priests and scholars. He was active in the religious discourse of his day, exchanging letters, poems, inscriptions, and other occasional writings with a wide range of colleagues and acquaintances, although not with persons of particularly great renown.[18]

At the age of ten or eleven, this bright young man had found himself fatherless and hence quite literally rootless. It is not surprising, then, that he left home to follow a Taoist master. Pai's journey began with a sense of loss, a literal uprooting from the foundations of his world. Although he established his own center, he continued to travel and to make connections with multiple religious streams and practices.

Another wanderer was Lin Chao-en (1517-1598), second son of an eminent and learned family from P'u-t'ien, Fukien. Lin Chao-en's family pedigree seemed to augur a life of enormous success and influence in the world of Chinese scholar-officials and the Fukien local elite. However, in his twenties, he lost his wife, his grandfather, and his father, all in the space of five years. At the age of thirty, he also lost his uncle, the rising star of the family and Lin's hope of sponsorship for making his way in the world. All of this precipitated a crisis for the young man, who abandoned studies for the official examinations and set off in search of the Way, spending several years in the rather dubious company of one Cho Wan-ch'un (flourished sixteenth century), a "disheveled Taoist" type. In this period, he visited a number of religious sites and masters, and in 1551 met an enlightened master (probably in a dream or a vision) who taught him the true Way. From this point on, he began to gather disciples and to function as a religious teacher, although his teachings and practices continued to evolve.[19]

Lin's journey into the religious life, like Pai Yü-ch'an's, was impelled by the loss of loved ones and also of those who could help him establish a foothold in Chinese elite society. Like Pai, he journeyed beyond the bounds (*fang-wai*) to find answers and meaning, and—having found them—began to gather around himself a community of disciples with whom he could establish a practice and curriculum which would help them to embody the principles of the Way.

Lin Chao-en did not remain separated from the world or his family. His relatives helped to edit and publish his writings and were involved in his religious organization. Lin Chao-en himself was justly famous in his home town for philanthropic work on behalf of the victims, living and dead, of Japanese pirate raids. His spiritual journey inspired him to offer a new teaching, a combination of what he considered to be the authentic aspects of the Three Teachings in a single religious movement (*san-chiao ho-i*, lit. Three Teachings combined in one). In Lin's system, Confucian, Buddhist, or Taoist groups would follow their distinctive teachings and practices and yet understand their underlying unity. Lin's vision embraced something from various paths or streams, and he brought them together and justified them with his distinctive rhetoric. His Way of the Three Teachings was a creative union of elements from many paths of the Chinese religious field into an ethical, meditative, and curative practice in Nine Stages.[20]

The stories of these two men illustrate important aspects of the religious path or journey. Both were moved to wander beyond the bounds by a personal loss or reversal. As they wandered beyond the bounds, their horizons were expanded and they were touched by multiple streams of Chinese religious tradition. It was in unlikely locations and from unlikely sources that they found their answers. Their journeys were marked by loss, followed by wandering in new and uncharted territory in the hopes of finding a sure foothold on the Way.

My own pilgrimage also had begun with loss: the loss of my cultural and religious center as my horizons expanded. In addition, my father had died unexpectedly while I was a freshman in college. An American who had come of age during the Second World War, my father had rather traditional expectations of my life as a woman; his death both freed and challenged me to chart a bolder course for my life. To find that course, I too wandered beyond the bounds, embracing exile from my Western culture in order to explore uncharted territories. In my pilgrimage in Chinese culture, I was touched by many streams of religious life and practice. Like the two men in these tales, I too found insights in unlikely places. And, like them, I learned the benefits of wandering, of being a pilgrim or seeker.

I identified with both of these stories, but most especially with the most famous story of Chinese pilgrimage, captured in the novel *Journey to the West*.

西
遊
記

Journey to the West

All of the themes of Chinese religious journey are brilliantly and enter-tainingly presented in Wu Ch'eng-en's (c. 1500-1582) novel *Journey to the West*, skillfully and perceptively translated by Anthony Yü.[21] This novel, first published in the late sixteenth century and immensely pop-ular in traditional China, is a tale of religious quest and pilgrimage. Paralleling the Chinese genius for developing layers and levels of reli-gious symbolism, the journey takes place at many levels.

At one level, the tale is a fictionalized account of the journey of the historical pilgrim Hsüan-tsang (c. 596-664), commissioned by the T'ang emperor to travel to India and return to China with the full range of Buddhist writings. Hsüan-tsang undertook a long and ardu-ous overland journey along the silk route, the steppes, and the moun-tains to India and back, passing through many cultures and realms along the way. Although an emissary of the T'ang emperor, Hsüan-tsang was also a pilgrim in his own right; the novel is an account of his spiritual growth.

In the novel, Hsüan-tsang (or Tripitika, as he is more frequently called) is accompanied by three companions who act as his guardians or champions—Old Monkey, Pa-chieh, and Sha Monk—each of whom has a monstrous or beastly appearance, symbolizing their need for spiritual refinement.[22] Like Dorothy's companions on her journey to Oz, these were unlikely, albeit endearing, champions. Despite their attainment of considerable spiritual powers, they had committed grievous sins which they sought to expiate through this pilgrimage, thereby purging their monstrous aspects. Thus the tale also recounts the pilgrimage of the three guardians or disciples. The tales of these three are raucous; their foibles are so apparent that readers laugh and at the same time recognize them as all too human. As each of these three makes progress on the journey, readers are comforted with the thought that even such obvious character flaws might be transcended by means of a commitment to the Way.

Along the physical journey, the four pilgrims encounter a stunning array of cultures and strange, sometimes hilarious, obstacles; they meet every kind of monster and demon imaginable and fight scores of battles. On the most external level, their successes in these battles chronicle their progress on the road. Yet in each of the battles, one or more of the pilgrims learn a deeper, inner lesson; thus inner progress and spiritual insight always accompany external victory.

On another level, the pilgrimage takes these characters through vir-tually every sort of Chinese religious practice. Along the way, they have ample opportunity to test the rules and boundaries of the religious field. Thus although at a very superficial level the structure of the pilgrimage is "Buddhist" (after all, it is a Buddhist monk commissioned by the emperor to seek Buddhist scriptures), it is fundamentally a journey through the entire Chinese religious landscape.

As the pilgrims progress, each achievement is challenged by a new danger and obstacle. As they grow in strength, faith, courage, and discernment, they are called upon to face greater challenges and to advance even further in the Way. Even after they finally reach their goal and request the scriptures, the Buddha's disciples give them wordless scriptures.[23] The Buddha of the Past recognizes,

> Most of the priests in the land of the East are so stupid and blind that they will not recognize the value of these wordless scriptures. When that happens, won't it have made this long trek of our sage monk completely worthless? (391)

In order not to discourage the "stupid and blind priests," the Buddha of the Past arranges for the four pilgrims to discover that the scriptures are empty and to trade the wordless scriptures for more conventional scriptures. Nonetheless, the point has been made: the true "dharma" is wordless, and the scriptures were not the ultimate prize. Thus this tale of religious quest serves as a brilliant depiction of the open-ended, never-final Way of Chinese religious life.

The novel is beloved by the Chinese as a witty, raucous story; the story is often depicted in popular forms (opera, cinema, even cartoons) for sheer entertainment, especially for children. At that level it functions as a kind of religious fairy tale, where the "good guys" finally win after overcoming all of the dangers. But the novel, like Lion's Head Mountain and Chinese religious teaching, offers layer upon layer of meaning, and one could wander through its pages numerous times, never failing to discover new insights.

An important meaning is that Tripitika had to leave the bounds of Chinese culture to make his pilgrimage; he had to wander beyond the bounds (*fang-wai*) in order to seek the Truth. Like Dorothy in *The Wizard of Oz*, he too ultimately returned home transformed.

Characteristically, his sojourn encompassed many levels:
- it was a historical pilgrimage from China to India and back;
- it could be read as an allegory of either Buddhist or Taoist practice;
- it incorporated myriad elements of the Chinese religious field and its many lessons;
- it embraced, interiorized, and then shed various levels of religious belief and practice;
- it was an interior journey toward self-awareness and self-transcendence;
- it related the conquest of various demonic and beastly powers within each person;

西
遊
記

- it satirized both religion and culture and simultaneously affirmed their deepest values.

Perhaps most importantly, however, it was a lesson about religious life *as* journey, for every time the pilgrims passed through one part of the journey, another opened before them, and what they believed they had obtained always turned out not to be the prize. It was the journey, and what each of the pilgrims learned on it, that comprised the Way. As it was for Dorothy and her companions, the journey was all.

Journey to the West adds significant dimensions to the Chinese concept of journey and to my understanding of my pilgrimage on Lion's Head Mountain. It teaches that even ordinary, fallible folk profit from the journey; those who undertake the journey learn from their experiences, from their failures as well as their triumphs. It underscores the profound notion that the point of the journey is not to achieve some goal or gain a prize. The journey *is* the pilgrim's progress. As I achieved one insight in my study of China, new vistas opened before me, promising further spiritual growth. Most profoundly, it encompasses all of the aspects of an intentional life (even the ridiculous and embarrassing) under the umbrella of the pilgrimage, or the Way. Spiritual progress is not always smooth and dignified; it is, however, the adventure of life.

Final Thoughts

Having learned from the Chinese something about their understanding of religious journey, I could discern more clearly the meaning of my own sojourn in Chinese culture. It was intellectual and cultural, yes; but it was much more. It was a pilgrimage which broadened my spiritual as well as cultural horizons. It was a journey of the spirit, which strengthened my spiritual life and health. It was a wandering beyond the bounds, a quest for a broader vision of my specific place in the spiritual landscape.

I sought in Chinese culture a remedy to my own former narrow cultural and religious vision, expiation for the sins of cultural and religious chauvinism and the attendant distrust and hatred of "the other." Seeking this remedy entailed the spiritual discipline of becoming an outsider,[24] an "other," as I had been in the South in 1955. I became an "other," both to learn from Chinese culture as a guest, and to learn an appropriate global humility, recognizing that my natal culture is not the norm of the entire world. Broadened cultural horizons required recognizing many centers in the human community, and broadened religious horizons required recognizing many vital religious communities. This spiritual discipline cultivated a healthier horizon. This form of spiritual journey has roots in my own heritage; in the images of the people of Israel wandering forty years in the wilderness before they reached the promised land or of Jesus' spending forty days in the wilderness in prayer. In my tradition, as in the Chinese, one is sometimes called to wander beyond the bounds in preparation for renewed vision or commitment.

Along the way, I was touched by many forms of religious life which enriched me or gave me new perspectives on my Christian heritage. The embracing of many levels of Chinese religion in the single path up Lion's Head Mountain and the stunning affirmation of many layers and levels of religiosity in *Journey to the West* presented a strikingly different approach to the many paths and practices of religion. I was inspired to learn from the Chinese an alternative way of understanding religious neighbors.

西
遊
記

CHAPTER 3

入

道

Forging a
New Path

Beyond the
Dilemma of the
Wider Ecumenism

[Hsüan-tsang] toured throughout the Western World for four-
teen years, going to all the foreign nations in quest of the
proper doctrines. He led the life of an ascetic beneath the twin
sâla trees and by the eight rivers of India. At the Deer Park
and on the Vulture Peak he attained strange visions. He re-
ceived ultimate truths from the senior sages and was taught
true doctrines by the highest worthies. . . . The multitudes,
once full of sins, are now brought back to blessing. Like that
which quenches the fire in a burning house, the power of
Buddhism works to save humanity lost on its way to perdi-
tion. Like a golden beam shining on darkened waters, it leads
the voyagers to climb the other shore safely.

—Wu Ch'eng-en
Journey to the West

The Buddhist pilgrim Hsüan-tsang traveled fourteen years to India
and back to bring the full panoply of Buddhist teachings to China. The
benefits of Hsüan-tsang's pilgrimage went beyond his own spiritual
maturity and that of his disciples; he also brought back to his native
land religious ideas, practices, and writings which benefited his people
and his community. Similarly, I write this book in the spirit of a pilgrim, bringing tales from my sojourn in China to my community.

"Entering the Path"
Entering the path or embarking on a journey or religious practice. In Chinese religious life, the most significant point is the beginning, as in the folk saying, "A journey of 10,000 miles begins with a single step."

I am by no means the first Christian writer to seek wisdom from other traditions. Many have gone before me, and I have learned from them. Popular writers like Alan Watts and Thomas Merton have long inspired Christian readers with the potential of combining or bringing into dialogue Asian and Christian spiritualities; that work is being continued today by scholars like Ruben Habito.[1] Scholars such as John Cobb and Abe Masao, not to mention a number of ongoing groups and societies, have been advancing inter-religious dialogues.[2] Robert Neville and Thomas Kasulis, among others, are pursuing comparative philosophy.[3] Alan Race, John Hick, Paul Knitter, and Francis Clooney are seeking to develop global theologies or comparative theologies.[4] I have profited from these colleagues, and deeply respect what they have achieved.

In this book I am addressing related but different issues. I am not asking about theological warrants or making arguments for openness to beliefs and practices of other religions; rather I am looking for attitudes and strategies by which Christians could live and interact more fruitfully with the members and institutions of other religious communities. I am joining in the conversation from my particular perspective and with my particular expertise. I do not intend to supplant what others have accomplished, but rather to open up a fresh approach to learning from our Asian neighbors, particularly with regard to the challenges and opportunities of living with religious diversity.

Religious diversity has been a particular nemesis for Christians because of the long historical habit of Christian exclusivism. Christian claims of universal and exclusive salvation create a set of dilemmas for those who seek to be open to their religious neighbors. In this chapter, I briefly recount those dilemmas and present my particular approach to them.

Christian Exclusivity

The Christian tradition of exclusivity is ancient and has been supported by passages from the Gospels, such as John 14:6: "I am the way, and the truth, and the life; no one comes to the Father, but by me." For the early church, a fragile movement struggling to establish itself among a plethora of religious options in the ancient Near East, insisting on a firm commitment to the community of faith was no doubt an important survival strategy, even more so in periods of persecution.

As the church became established and state-sponsored, however, claims of exclusivity became a justification for enforcing conformity (orthodoxy) as opposed to allowing nonconformity (heresy or apostasy),[5] or for conquering and converting "heathen" lands, thereby saving the souls of the inhabitants.

Challenges to Exclusivity

Assumptions of exclusivity began to be challenged as Western Christians from the mid-nineteenth century on developed fuller knowledge of world religions and cultures. Such knowledge helped "erode the plausibility of the old Christian exclusivism."[6] As the European colonial system crumbled after World War II, Christian and non-Christian groups throughout the world raised their voices to challenge the assumptions and parochialism of Western Christians and their complicity in colonialism.[7]

These challenges to assumptions of Christian exclusivism have sparked a debate within Christianity about its relationship to other religions. The debate currently rages under the rubric of the "wider ecumenism."[8] Alan Race has grouped current Christian stances toward other religions into three categories: exclusivist, inclusivist, and pluralist.[9]

In Race's typology, exclusivists argue for the uniqueness and superiority of the Christian path to salvation and basically affirm that "outside of the Christian faith, there is no salvation." Although the dominance of this position is eroding, it has had a long history and still colors the attitudes of many Christians.

Inclusivists concede that adherents of other religions experience the grace of God and may find salvation outside of the Christian faith, but still maintain the superiority of the Christian way to salvation. Those who find God in other traditions are "anonymous Christians" (Rahner) or have experienced a vestige of Christian revelation through some other form. Ultimately, in this life or the next, those practicing other faiths will find their full salvation *as Christians*. Critics have noted the condescension of this view toward the adherents of other traditions who would not welcome seeing themselves as anonymous Christians, any more than Christians would welcome being seen as, say, anonymous Muslims.

Pluralists affirm that there are a diversity of legitimate religious faiths and paths to salvation. Some, like John Hick, argue that the many faiths are all responses to one Ultimately Real, and that the differences among them reflect not only the limitations of human language and cultural constructions of faith, but also the specific historical conditions in which those faiths have emerged.[10] Hick challenges Christians to rethink their fundamental theological categories in such areas as Christology and atonement in order to open Christianity to the truths and ways of other religious traditions.[11] He proposes a philosophy of religion and a reading of Christian theology which can embrace the full range of religious diversity.

In general terms, exclusivists fortify and protect the boundaries of Christianity, upholding its distinctive message as the only viable way to salvation. Inclusivists provide a cautious opening to other traditions, embracing them under the Christian umbrella, while preserving the unique saving power of the gospel message. Pluralists push hardest at the boundaries, seeking a way to re-envision Christianity as one religion among many peer religions.

All three positions imply a strategy for living with religious neighbors. The exclusivists would opt at best for peaceful coexistence, arguing that "good fences make good neighbors." They pray for and work towards the conversion of all peoples to the gospel of Christianity. The inclusivists affirm other religions as disguised forms of Christianity; they cautiously welcome neighbors from other religious communities, seeing their distinctive practices as underdeveloped forms of Christianity.[12] The pluralist approach is genuinely open to interacting with other religious communities as neighbors and equals, and thus would seem to have some promise for the issues discussed in this volume. This approach merits a closer look.

The Pluralist Approach

Two recent volumes capture fairly well the current discussions in pluralist theology. *The Myth of Christian Uniqueness: Toward a Pluralistic Theology of Religions*,[13] edited by John Hick and Paul Knitter, is derived from a conference at the School of Theology at Claremont in 1986. *Christianity and the Wider Ecumenism*,[14] edited by Peter Phan, is based on papers from a 1988 conference sponsored by the Council for the World's Religions in Istanbul, Turkey. Both conferences were conversations about Christian attitudes toward world religions among Christians who had devoted considerable time and energy to interfaith dialogue. North American voices dominated, although both conferences included representatives from other continents, including Europe, Africa, and Asia. These two volumes push steadily at the boundaries of Christian parochialism. They make a number of claims about why the issue of pluralism must engage contemporary Christians.

Langdon Gilkey argues that a pluralist approach to Christianity is a necessary adjustment to the end of the unquestioned dominance of Western culture and the Christian religion.[15]

Stanley Samartha argues that Christians must attend to the negative impact of exclusivist attitudes on non-Western cultures. He admonishes:

> Theological claims have political consequences. This is particularly true in contemporary India where the exclusive claims made by any one particular community of faith affects its relationships with members of other communities of faith. . . .

Such claims, open or hidden, also raise basic theological questions concerning God's relationship to the whole of humanity, not just to one stream of it.[16]

If Christians hope to establish a presence in cultures like India's, they will have to watch their attitudes toward other religions and send messages consistent with the gospel to which they witness.

In these volumes, Christians who have discovered "elements of openness [which] pulsate throughout the biblical witness, contending with contrary impulses of ethno-centrism and religious imperialism,"[17] seek to explore and correct the errors of exclusivistic readings of the Bible, and to point to what can be learned from inter-religious scriptural interpretation.[18] Some follow Hick in attempting to revalorize traditional Christian theological categories in ways more open to the pluralism of religions.[19] Others look to modern theological writings to find a theological base in the church for openness.[20] Seiichi Yagi turns to a Buddhist theologian/philosopher for constructive help in understanding the relation of divine and human in the person of Jesus.[21] Others revisit the history of the Christian church to understand the intentions and limitations of attacks on "those outside the faith."[22] The liberationists find in the search for justice a possible common ground among the world's religions, or at least an opening for such a ground.[23]

One sees in these writers an emergent vision of Christianity, continuous with tradition, but open to the religious diversity of the world in which we live. One also sees an unfinished struggle with the still-dominant exclusivistic attitudes within Christianity. Even the pluralists themselves are not entirely comfortable with all moves proposed, fearing that some may threaten the integrity of Christian faith. Peter Phan, who edited one of these volumes, criticizes the pluralists for being a bit too open in their Christology.

> This imperceptible slippage from Christianity to Jesus, whether intentional or not, is, in my opinion, the Achilles' heel of the pluralist stance, for, and this is my contention, while it is not possible to claim that Christianity is unique in the sense of definitive, absolute, normative, and superior to other religions, it is legitimate to claim that Jesus is the only Christ and Savior.[24]

Phan is thus implicitly critical of John Hick's celebration of a "metaphorical Christology," where Jesus' divinity is not ontological, but inspirational.[25]

Mary Ann Stenger has captured the dilemma that many in the pluralist camp experience.

入
道

> Many of us grew up with [an exclusivistic] "Christian" out-
> look, but today we are uncomfortable with the imperialism of
> such an approach which often went hand in hand with
> economic and political imperialism. From a popular, liberal
> standpoint, some resolve this discomfort by rejecting all
> efforts at conversion and saying, "To each, his/her own." But if
> we look at this stance more deeply, we are also dissatisfied
> with an unthought-out pure relativism.[26]

Thus many Christians who seek openness to other religions and
who engage in inter-religious dialogue fear that the theological moves
of the pluralists go too far, undermining the very heart of what it
means to be Christian. Paul Knitter perceptively comments:

> All of these reservations, which come not from the Falwells
> and Ratzingers but from some of the more liberal thinkers in
> our communities, are based on the perceived clash between
> the new nonabsolute views of Christ and the *sensus fidelium*.
> So, if these new christologies [nonabsolute views of Christ]
> have any future within Christian theology, they need a better
> *ecclesial mediation* in order that they might be "received" by
> the faithful.[27]

early stages still

The pluralist position is in an early process of development and is
still sorting through debates about the dangers and limits of its various moves. Some of the reservations concern the preservation of the
distinctive integrity of Christianity and building an ecclesial foundation for the new openness; others concern the potentially unhappy
implications of relativism or pluralism as ends in themselves.

Mark Heim has raised another level of concern about the pluralist
position, exposing a potentially profound contradiction in the argu-   *uhh...*
ments of pluralists who insist that all religions are "fundamentally" the
same. He wonders whether their rush to affirm the compatability of
religions masks a worry about conversion, about genuine and significant change in religious affiliation. He writes, "We could consider
another possibility. Perhaps it is not difference that is the primary
source of tension but the dynamic of religious change itself. Does the
core difficulty rest not in the recognition of differences among the traditions but in the life option of migration among them?"[28] As Heim
points out, in the contemporary world more and more people "are born
into cultures that contain multiple religious options."[29] Thus one's religious affiliation is less a given, less a certainty, than in premodern
times. The pluralists, by denying the "real" or "significant" differences
among religions, he argues, render the significance of conversion null,
and thus make it less attractive. Genuine pluralism, he argues, would

*Religious affiliation = murky more now
than ever*

入
道

recognize the significant differences among religions, recognizing fully that each considers itself the only true way. In other words, it would develop a theology of multiple religious truths or alternatives.

Francis Clooney's important book *Seeing through Texts* argues for close, detailed, multifaceted, linguistically informed theological studies of other traditions to lay a groundwork for sober, careful comparison. Acknowledging that similarities unearthed will tempt one to make comparisons, he sounds a note of caution:

> From the very beginnings of such comparisons, though, we need to recognize that much will have already been done to make them plausible, likely to succeed, just by the prior decisions made in the identification of such possibilities. Any such comparison must be moderated by a lively sense of how each side of the comparison fits—theologically, textually, culturally, etc.—with its entire context, and where we are standing when we observe these materials together. It is helpful to undertake such comparisons with the expectation of always doing more of them, trying other kinds of comparisons as well: of concepts, poetic texts, excerpts from treatises, ethical norms, ritual enactments, festivals, etc. If one crosses the religious boundary intelligently, no single comparison can be decisive, even if one determines with a rare degree of certitude that in this or that instance either similarities or differences are preponderant.[30]

Clooney argues for deferring the move to creating a comparative theology, in order both to continue correcting one's understanding through further scholarship, and also to examine more deeply the agenda one brings to the endeavor and the appropriate resistances representatives of the other tradition might have to that agenda. He notes that the building of a meaningful encompassing narrative which included both traditions would require the establishment of a new religious community, committed to both, for whom that narrative would be meaningful.[31] The cautions raised in this book merit thoughtful attention, as does the groundbreaking scholarship which deepens the foundation for the possibility of a comparative theology.

Affirming Particularity and Openness

As a historian of religions, I bring another level of analysis to the debates within the pluralist movement. Seen from the standpoint of comparative religious patterns, pluralists, as they seek to redress the exclusivistic excesses of Christian history, run the danger of neglecting a vital aspect of religious affiliation and identity: its particularizing role in establishing identity and social location.

Anthropologists and historians of religion have long noted that religion is one means—along with language, dress, dietary habits, social customs, music, dance, and others—by which human groups situate themselves among a range of possibilities in the world; religion is one of the ways communities define a home base, a center, a distinctive identity and location. In some societies all of these markers define the social boundaries between one community and a neighboring one; in modern societies, these markers locate one's "own" in the complex social landscape.

Alice Walker, a leading African-American woman novelist, writes movingly of her discovery of a religious and communal bond while reading the stories of Zora Neale Hurston, a pioneer African-American author:

> I will never forget, reading Zora, and seeing for the first time, written down, the prayer that my father, and all the old elders before him, prayed in church. The one that thanked God that the cover on his bed the night before was not his winding sheet, nor his bed itself his cooling board. . . . Reading her, I saw for the first time, my own specific culture, and recognized it as such, with its humor always striving to be equal to its pain, and I felt as if, indeed, I had been given a map that led to the remains of my literary country.[32]

It is striking that the "literary country" was marked as hers by the prayer her father prayed; religion establishes powerful markers of identity, and sustains and transmits the distinctive traditions of the community. It is part of the map of each community's distinctive territory of meaning and practice.

While the history of humankind makes it abundantly clear that this role of religion in establishing social location and boundaries can give rise to the horrific abuses of religious persecution, oppression, and violence against "the other," denying the importance of this aspect of religion creates other problems. If the human world were simply a vast marketplace of ideas, practices, beliefs, and mores with no boundaries and no identifiable communities of meaning, we would all be adrift in a sea of anomie and would have no place from which to establish relationships. The Catholic Theological Union in Chicago, committed to nurturing a global perspective in theology and ministry, sees a secure Christian identity as the indispensable foundation of the "global person":

[A] global person is understood as someone who is secure in personal, cultural, and religious identity. Freed by this security, a global person does not need to prejudice or dismiss others because of their identity. A global person shows qualities of being humble and of open-minded disposition, has empathy and the ability to show solidarity with the oppressed and the marginalized. A global person is able to enter into relations of mutuality and interdependence with the oppressed and marginalized as well as building bridges with systems and members of the dominant society.[33]

The particularizing aspect of religion locates persons among the world of possibilities. Religion also has a counterbalancing aspect which pulls toward relationship with other communities and opens us to new experiences. Anthropologists, folklorists, and historians of religion thrive on tracing the diffusions, cultural influences, and adaptations of motifs, practices, and tales which cross the lines of religions and cultures. Religious communities absorb and adapt images, tales, and practices from their neighbors as a way of enriching and developing their community life: whether it is Babylonian myths finding their way into the book of Genesis; the influence of early mystery cults and other religions on the Christian practice of baptism and the celebrations of Christmas and Easter; or the absorption of local practices and motifs in the "universal" religions of Buddhism, Christianity, and Islam as they spread and take root in diverse cultures around the world. Often the external elements are absorbed in a friendly way without impacting central teachings and practices, as in the cases cited above. At other times, the external element is seen as a challenge to religious beliefs and practices of the community, and it must be incorporated into a revised and expanded sense of religious life in order to safeguard the future of the community. Not only do religious communities and cultures establish ways to mark themselves off from one another, they also interact and borrow from their neighbors.

Moreover, religious communities establish transcendent spiritual and ethical ideals which point beyond the current practices and achievements of the community to a more demanding, holier ideal. This spiritual idealism can open the community to new experiences and realizations, to discovering a limitation or even an error in some previous "given" of the community. For example, if John 14:6 is frequently cited by Christians in favor of exclusivist views, an equally strong biblical case can be made for openness to the stranger and love for the neighbor. Durwood Foster has written an essay in *Christianity and the Wider Ecumenism* articulating sound biblical warrants for ecumenical and interfaith openness.[34] Christianity, like most religions, has both a boundary-setting, exclusivist side, and a broader, more open aspect.

The interplay of the opening and boundary-setting dimensions of religious life is of crucial importance to the flourishing of human civilization. Without a clear sense of identity and a community of identification, we can find no place to stand in a vast and challenging world. We lose our center, and the world slips from a meaning-filled cosmos into a demonic chaos.[35] Without an openness to our neighbors, on the other hand, we are cut off from vast reserves of human creativity for the nurture of human life. The exclusivists stress the particularizing side, the pluralists the open aspects of Christianity. As a historian of religions, I would argue that both aspects will have to be honored if Christianity is going to continue to flourish in the global and multireligious world. The issue is, how to find the balance.

A New Path

The pluralist theologians have recovered in the Bible, and in Christian history and doctrine, foundations for a less exclusive and more open version of Christianity. They have done important work, but have frequently run up against long-standing patterns of Christian interpretation, history, and thinking dominated by exclusivist assumptions. Progress toward a less exclusive and more open version of Christianity will inevitably be very slow, because of the need for ecclesial mediation.

Diana Eck has opened a new and very promising path in her excellent book *Encountering God: A Spiritual Journey from Bozeman to Banaras*.[36] Eck is an Indologist and historian of religions by training, and a church woman with extensive experience in interfaith work. Her book, like mine, recounts tales from her spiritual and intellectual journey, bringing the voices and views of her Hindu and other non-Christian friends and colleagues to her readers, and also sharing her conversations with fellow Christians about the potential for Christian openness.

Eck's book centers around the notion of God as having many forms and levels, encountered by following many paths. The theme is aptly chosen, for it represents brilliantly the Indian/Hindu approach to religious diversity. She creates with and for her readers a profound respect for the genuine religious faith and life of others, and for their extraordinary vision of the multiplicity of God. I warmly commend this book to those who have not already read it.

My approach is closer to Eck's than to the pluralist theologians, but it follows yet another path. I do not seek to forge an ecumenical theology, nor to find biblical, ecclesial, or doctrinal warrants for openness to Asian religions. I do not seek to persuade the North American Christian community of any compatibility of belief, doctrine, or approach, or even that "God" can be found in Chinese religions, although that is certainly my experience.

As one who has sojourned extensively along the paths of Chinese religions, it is my observation and experience that relations with other religions are more readily built upon practice and symbols than on doctrine and scripture.[37] In saying this I do not denigrate the importance of engaging doctrinal and scriptural issues; I simply acknowledge that such a path is long and rocky, best traversed by specialists willing to invest considerable time in studying the scriptures, traditions, and theologies of other religions.

If doctrine and scripture are stumbling blocks to our interactions with other religions, symbol and practice can bypass some of these road blocks. The inter-religious accessibility of symbols is evidenced in the power of religious art to inspire persons from outside of the faith. Art has long been an important proselytizing and inspirational tool of religious communities. In addition, the mutual accessibility of spiritual practice may rest on one of several grounds. Practices of different faiths may seem familiar, and thus draw the interest of another group. One example is the case of Vietnamese Buddhists joining the Portuguese Catholics' saints day celebration, cited at the beginning of chapter 1.[38]

The practices of another community can also provide a new avenue for expressing spirituality.[39] Thus some Christians have studied Zen meditation techniques as a way of nurturing their Christian contemplative life; Protestant groups have held retreats with leaders specializing in Benedictine spirituality.[40] Finally, practices of another community can open one's vistas to new horizons of spiritual expression in a particular dimension of life. I, for instance, was deeply moved by the Chinese practice of reporting to the ancestors events and decisions in the life of the family, maintaining the communication link with deceased loved ones. This practice gave me a spiritual venue for extending into my adult life the relationship with my deceased father.

Such spiritual practices can be relatively easily assimilated into one's religious life without requiring that all of the attendant theological and ecclesial issues be addressed or even acknowledged, although they do raise such issues as they are entered into more deeply.[41] Such accommodations simply reflect our ability to learn from others and to adapt our behavior. They are, at least at the outset, a path of little resistance and few obstacles. The problem is that, until such practices come to be understood in their full context, the authentic interfaith issues have not been addressed; it is at this moment that the more difficult (yet more promising) issues come to the fore.

This book, then, takes another path. From traditional China I bring accounts of religious patterns and practices, of strategies for living with religious diversity day by day. These are not offered as a model for North American Christian life, since the accounts represent cultural patterns from a distant time and place, a context which no longer exists. These accounts do, however, function as a mirror; they pose a fascinating alternative to the Western story of religious exclusivity and sectarianism. In recounting the tales from traditional China, I use the tools and perspectives of the historian of Chinese religions, recounting ways in which another culture has met these issues and addressed them quite differently than in the West.

The historian of religions begins with observation of religious life and behavior in a variety of cultures. She notes patterns of religious behavior, commonalities and differences, and noteworthy strategies. She places similar examples in juxtaposition, to allow for comparison and contrast. Comparative analysis brings out aspects of all examples which are not obvious when they are viewed in isolation. It challenges and stretches culturally embedded assumptions and categories of analysis, highlighting both the distinctiveness of each example and what each neglects or suppresses. Comparisons of patterns of religious life refine powers of observation and analysis, so that one begins to see more clearly how members of a religious community shape their traditions through selective observance.

In this book, I assume the voice of a pilgrim. No mere observer, I seek to bring out, in the stories which I select and the way in which I recount them, those aspects of Chinese religious life that strike me as edifying. I deliberately intersperse stories in which I recount from first-hand experience—narrating events through my distinctive interpretive lens—with stories which surprised me or challenged me to see things in a very different Chinese way. In these latter, I seek to convey faithfully the perspectives and lenses of the Chinese narrators, even though (and because) this stretches both my horizons and those of my readers. I find in China a remarkably textured pattern of religious life which offers striking alternative approaches to religious diversity.

The strategies and attitudes of traditional China are not a panacea; the remarkable patterns which are noted here began to break down as internal and external pressures crumbled the very foundations of traditional Chinese culture. The Chinese cannot go back to those lost days, and the West certainly cannot model itself on the Chinese imperial system. Although Chinese culture does not have all the answers to the challenge of religious diversity, these stories offer a fascinating alternative scenario to the history of religious sectarianism and competition in Western countries.

The stories I tell of China pose the following questions, and more.

- What happens if a society starts from the premise that multiple religious affiliations are *normal*?
- What happens if religious organizations are hospitable to one another in order to create and sustain the larger community?
- What happens if a culture develops patterns to create and sustain mutual familiarity and regular interaction among members of various religious groups?

These stories have given me a fresh perspective on the history and patterns of religious life in my culture; I hope they may do so for others. I also hope that they will help us to recognize and recover in our own cultural heritage traditions of hospitality, generosity, and mutual respect. These may become the foundations for exhibiting more open attitudes toward religious neighbors, while at the same time building vital communities of faith and practice which can serve as effective spiritual centers for persons and families in our richly diverse society.

PART 2

Tales of Chinese Religious Diversity

CHAPTER 4

Diversity and Competition in the Chinese Religious Field

Filial piety can dissolve all the calamities of life.
If we practice filial piety toward our aged parents,
This is the equivalent of opening (and reading) the sutras all
day. . . .
If we wish to emulate the upright characteristics of the Bud-
dha, then there is nothing that can surpass filial piety.
—*Yüan-chien*
                    Erh-shih-ssu-hsiao ya-tso-wen

As a pilgrim on Lion's Head Mountain, I saw clearly that the Chinese envisioned their diverse religious traditions as part of a single Way. However, given my long-ingrained habits of exclusivist thinking about religion, I found myself repeatedly surprised and confused by Chinese inclusivism. While I could celebrate the general idea as an alternative to Western religious sectarianism and intolerance, I could not grasp the implications of shifting to an inclusivist perspective; I just couldn't "get it" at first, as much as I wanted to. I was, in the initial stages of my pilgrimage, considerably slowed by my difficulties in grasping the inclusivist perspective.

Take the epigraph to this chapter. What is Yüan-chien, a T'ang dynasty (618-907) Buddhist monk, doing claiming that filial piety (a cardinal Confucian value) is the best way to practice Buddhism? Yüan-chien's Buddhist paean to filial piety is an excellent example of

---

"Well"
The character for well is the symbol of the well-field system, which is one image used in the chapter to represent the Chinese religious field.

crossover and mutual borrowing among various religious groups in China. Yüan-chien, as we shall see later in the chapter, is not simply combining elements from two traditions important in his religious life; he is defending the place of Buddhism in Chinese religious life. He is pledging his allegiance, as it were, to the inclusive religious system of China.

This Chinese cultural practice of religious crossover is the antithesis of historical Christian patterns of exclusivity. It is grounded in a history of religious interaction very different from that which characterized Christianity in Europe and North America. That real and significant difference, that "otherness," held the promise of my pilgrimage, but also raised serious obstacles of understanding which I would have to overcome.

For instance, like virtually all Western scholars of Chinese religion (until very recently), my exclusivistic lenses distorted my perceptions so that I seriously misread the Chinese categories of the Three Teachings (Confucianism, Buddhism, and Taoism). Viewing the Three Teachings through Western lenses, we Western scholars saw the Three Teachings as independent, competing religions.[1] We were blind to the actual dynamics of the Chinese religious system.

This chapter will begin with the story of religious pluralism in China as we have gradually come to understand it. It is a story which challenges exclusivistic biases and assumptions.

As I became more and more aware of the inclusivistic patterns of religious pluralism in China, I was moved to develop a heuristic model which would help me and others from my culture to establish a framework on which to envision and understand the inclusive dynamics of religious pluralism. The second part of the chapter will develop that heuristic model.

As I became more familiar with the patterns and strategies that characterized religious pluralism, I also had to grow beyond my initial idealism, my delight in discovering "inclusivity." I learned that the patterns of Chinese inclusivity were intricately embedded in the patterns and dynamics of the culture. Like the religious history of the West, Chinese religious history was embroiled in politics, patronage, and power. If religion is to be part of "real life," it is inevitably implicated in the webs of social interaction and competition. The third part of the chapter recounts the entry and assimilation of a foreign religion, namely Buddhism, into Chinese culture. This tale illustrates well the dynamics of inclusivity, and the forces shaping and constraining it.

The Story of Religious Pluralism in China

From the earliest traces of human civilization, the territory which came to be China yielded a wealth of religious beliefs and practices:

mythological images, symbols, and stories; divination arts; elaborate
burial and funerary practices; shamanistic and demon-exorcising rites;
schema for understanding and ordering the cosmos. As religious ideas
evolved, they also developed into multiple streams which later came to
be labeled "Confucian," "Taoist," and "Buddhist." In reality, however,
there were numerous currents within each of those larger rivers, and
some tributaries which flowed beyond them; the banks between the
streams and tributaries were porous and changeable.

There were, from the outset, religious tensions in China: genuine
philosophical differences, rival rituals and pantheons, jockeying for
patronage of the wealthy and powerful, attempts by local and national
officials to domesticate the religious impulse.[2] Yet despite these very
real tensions and rivalries, the dominant story of religious pluralism
in China was one of tolerance of all teachings in the realm under
Heaven (*T'ien-hsia*). Like modern-day Japanese whose religious affiliations in the 1983 census added up to nearly twice the total population,[3] virtually all Chinese participated in more than one religion in
the course of their lifetimes, sometimes sequentially and sometimes
simultaneously. The Chinese state affirmed the multiplicity of religious groups and practices. Chinese imperial governments, like European monarchies, reserved to themselves the right to establish
religious orthodoxy and orthopraxy, and to declare any religious book
or practice illegal on the grounds that it threatened morals or state
security. Although the state had a strong bias for establishmentarian
religious beliefs and practices, it primarily sought to control religious
life by bringing it under the patronage, sponsorship, and support of
local and national officials. The Chinese state did not adopt a single
official religious teaching, but rather cast itself as the patron and protector of all legitimate forms of religion.

The Many Streams of Chinese Religious Life

In an attempt to impose some order in the Chinese religious world, the
labels "Confucian," "Buddhist," and "Taoist" were adopted by Han
dynasty (206 B.C.E.-202 C.E.) historians as classifications for writings,
biographies, and temples or shrines. Leaders of religious movements
came to use these labels polemically as each sought to differentiate his
movement from key contemporaries. Government authorities used the
labels to classify religious movements and practices for the purposes
of patronage and control.

Traditionally, the label "Confucian" was applied to those who took
as their canonical writings the *Four Books* ("The Great Learning,"
"The Doctrine of the Mean," and the writings of Confucius [551-479
B.C.E.] and Mencius [372?-289? B.C.E.]), as well as the *Thirteen Classics*.[4] Confucian thinkers focused on ethical and political issues, seek-

ing to identify the learning and practices which were the basis of a moral life and harmonious society.

"Taoist" was applied to four classes of writers: 1) philosophers who looked back to the writings of Lao Tzu (6th or 3rd c. B.C.E.), Chuang Tzu (369? - 286? B.C.E.), or the "Neo-Taoists"[5]; 2) thinkers in one of many ritual lineages of Taoism[6]; 3) specialists in forms of Taoist meditation (particularly Inner Alchemy) or in the arts of nurturing long life[7]; 4) and persons associated with temples designated as Taoist *kuan*. Taoist philosophers (both classical and Neo-Taoist) reflected on the Way of nature, and on the principle of the natural or spontaneous (*tzu-jan*) as an approach to human life. Ritual Taoists learned to introject spirits in order to heal, exorcise, or comfort souls. Meditative Taoists taught the reintegration of the fragmented self through a process of returning to original unity. Practitioners of the arts of long life practiced medicine, *t'ai-ch'i*, alchemy, or other occult arts.

"Buddhists" based their teachings on Buddhist scriptures and practices, originally transmitted from various Buddhist schools in India or Tibet, but later refined and developed in China. The Chinese ultimately developed their own distinctive forms of Buddhism in the Pure Land and Ch'an traditions. Buddhists taught enlightenment or salvation through cultivation of insight (*kuan*) and quiescence (*chih*) by means of a variety of ritual and meditative practices or by faith in Buddhas and Bodhisattvas who would aid the faithful in their cultivation of the Buddhist Way.[8]

Published lineages of religious texts (which identified certain schools of thought), lineages of masters or teachers, esoteric ritual practices performed only by certain lineages of priests, and schools of interpretation of classical texts—all of these served as markers of distinct religious movements or schools in China. These divisions, while significant, also evolved over time, and as they did religious boundaries were redrawn and traditions reconfigured, as reshapers of one tradition borrowed liberally from others motifs, symbols, practices, and even deities.[9] Often this borrowing honored the teachings of other traditions in a friendly spirit; in other cases it was a form of competition through co-optation and expansion into a rival's religious terrain. The borders between groups were by no means absolute, and—most significantly—their devotees, patrons, and even occasionally their religious professionals overlapped and crossed boundaries. As C. K. Yang has noted,

> In popular religious life it was the moral and magical functions of the cults, and not the delineation of the boundary of religious faiths, that dominated people's consciousness. Even priests in some country temples were unable to reveal the identity of the religion to which they belonged. Centuries of

mixing gods from different faiths into a common pantheon had produced a functionally oriented religious view that relegated the questions of religious identify to a secondary place.[10]

In addition, the plethora of local and popular traditions do not neatly fall under any of the three labels, Confucian, Buddhist, or Taoist. As such practices grew they were sometimes classified or misclassified as belonging to one of the three teachings, but the fact remains that a vast portion of Chinese religious life was centered around local deities or practices; the labels "Confucian," "Buddhist," or "Taoist" are simply not helpful in these cases.[11]

An Alternative Model for Conceptualizing Chinese Religious Life

For these reasons, it is inadequate to think of Chinese religious life and practice as comprised of three separate, distinct, and competing religions called Confucianism, Buddhism, and Taoism. We need to take into account that religious communities both overlapped and competed with each other, drawing from a common pool of religious images, texts, symbols, and practices.

In order to facilitate such understanding, I employ the notion of Chinese religious field as a heuristic device to convey the patterns, interactivity, and permeability of Chinese religious practices and communities. The concept of religious field helped me to grasp the realities of Chinese religious pluralism in a number of ways.

First, it reminds me of the common pool of elements from which religious communities were free to draw. The Chinese religious field can be depicted in a number of ways: one is in terms of the idealized system of the agricultural "well-field" (*ching-t'ien*), described in the *Classic of Rites* (*Li Chi*), and invoked by Chinese reformers over the centuries as a remedy against the evils of excessive government centralization and taxation. The idea is based on the "tic-tac-toe" structure of the character *ching* (well) (see figure 4.1).

Figure 4.1

Mencius describes the system:

> Each well-field unit is one *li* square and contains nine hundred *mu* of land. The center lot is the public field. The eight households each own a hundred-*mu* farm and collaborate on cultivating the public field. When the public field has been properly attended, then they may attend to their own work.[12]

The well-field system, although it may never have been implemented in China, was invoked as an ideal because 1) it gave each family a plot of land for their support, and 2) it provided a localized system of self-help in lieu of central government taxation. It represented a utopian society where everyone had sufficient land and strong central government was superfluous.

I invoke this notion of field for the Chinese religious system because it metaphorically equalizes the various religious groups which surround the public field or common pool. At the center of the religious field, in my use of the metaphor, is a public or common pool of religious elements and motifs from which local institutions may draw (see figure 4.2). This field functioned primarily locally, for each locality had its distinctive set of temples and practices honoring local deities and teachers.[13] They might import elements of neighboring regions, be visited by teachers from afar, or collect texts which represented broader teachings. If these external elements were to have lasting impact, however, they would be incorporated into the local religious field.

Figure 4.2

At a second level, the metaphor of religious field can be depicted as a grid in which each local religious temple or shrine finds its appropriate niche (see figure 4.3). Chinese temples and deities in any given locale tend to sort themselves into complementary functions and ritual specializations, each developing a particular niche or location in the religious field. Moreover, the round of community festivals, rotating among the established religious temples and groups, creates a complementarity of religious patronage in the community. Local residents learn the powers and specializations of each shrine or deity, and approach them accordingly. Local elites develop patterns of religious patronage which express their leadership role in the community. Thus the field of local religious institutions has two distinct dimensions: 1) it reflects the social hierarchy of the community through the patterns of patronage, and 2) it establishes a range of complementary religious powers to protect and sustain the community. The grid aspect of the Chinese religious field is similar to the notion of religious field developed by Stanley Tambiah to analyze the relationship of Buddhism to Thai spirit cults.[14]

If the notion of Chinese religious field embraces the notion of the public field or common pool of religious elements, and of field as a grid in which each religious group finds its appropriate niche, the Chinese religious field must also have a dynamic or active aspect, for it is a field of religious interaction. Here religious leaders vie for patronage, seeking to strengthen their position on the local religious field. Here the laity seek instruction, boons, and ritual succor from

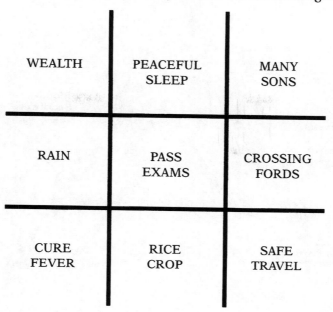

WEALTH	PEACEFUL SLEEP	MANY SONS
RAIN	PASS EXAMS	CROSSING FORDS
CURE FEVER	RICE CROP	SAFE TRAVEL

Figure 4.3

local religious resources, flocking to those deities or teachers who could deliver spiritual boons. People look to religion to further their fortunes, secular (health and wealth) and sacred (progress on the Way).

The Chinese religious field is a field of action, a playing field (or, if you will, a religious treasure hunt)[15] or a field of socio-economic competition. The latter builds on the notions of Pierre Bourdieu, who sought to reconcile the ideas of Durkheim, Marx, and Weber in an original theoretical model which could: 1) describe the contribution of religious institutions and practices to the perpetuation of social structure; 2) articulate the various pressures on religious institutions and leaders to compete as effective producers and distributors of religious goods; and 3) identify the role of socio-economic circumstances in shaping the views and needs of the groups to whom religious goods are delivered.[16] The play on the Chinese religious field takes place in the complex socio-economic web which Bourdieu seeks to model. In the analysis of this book, however, I will concentrate on four levels of interaction: 1) attempts by the state, both local and national, to control religious activity; 2) activities of local groups and leadership to assert their own interests in the religious field; 3) the role of religious leadership in developing and shaping religious traditions; and 4) the mechanisms through which the faithful learn about and take advantage of religious resources.

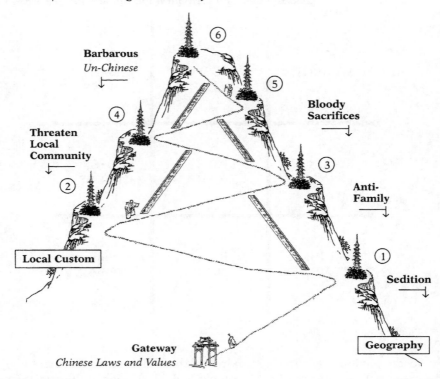

Figure 4.4

Since the Chinese have no tradition of competitive games on play-ing fields (unless one counts mahjong or chess), the dynamic aspect of the Chinese religious field is best visualized as a path on a mountain (See figure 4.4). Most local religious fields had a pilgrimage site (a mountain where available), and so this visualization builds on a solid Chinese tradition of representing a comprehensive vision of the reli-gious field. Pilgrimage sites or major temples display a vision of the religious field which includes many religious groups and deities, each in the proper place accorded to them by the host temple. For some religious groups, the best pilgrimage site is a steep mountain, as they would portray the religious field as demanding and their own tradi-tion as offering the best way to complete the challenge journey. For others, the mountain would have to be much more level, more accessi-ble, for they offer a version of the Way that is easy and open to all. Thus their version of the mountain would be a small hill, or even a level plain. Those of us living in the information age might want to think of figure 4.4 as a computer model in which the steepness of the mountain can be adjusted, according to which group is presenting the religious field.

Figure 4.4 suggests a path up a mountain representing the local religious field. The path is long and winding, wending its way through the variety of traditions represented in the local field (depicted as shrines 1-6). The narrow bridges between paths are ritual or meditative short-cuts advocated by some particular leader or group. These bridges can speed one along the Way but, like all short-cuts, have attendant dangers, and thus require spiritual assistance. (For those schools offering an easier path, these bridges might be elevators, or they would become easy strolls across a small stream.)

Although the path through the religious field encompasses considerable diversity, it does have its boundaries. The gate at the bottom represents Chinese (state) law and Chinese values (embodied in the classics). Without accepting these, one cannot enter the field. One can fall from the path into danger (heresy) by means of religious acts or beliefs which go beyond the bounds of the religious field: those that threaten the local community or are viewed as seditious by the state; those which are religiously offensive (bloody sacrifice or cannibalism); those practices which are outside the purview of Chinese civilization (i.e., barbarous); those which destroy the fabric of society (anti-family practices).

What complicates the visualization of the religious field is that in many locales, where more than one religious group competed for dominance, these strong groups each had their own picture of the shape of the whole, or the place of each shrine on the path and the location of effective short-cuts. What they shared was a notion that the religious field embraced the religious diversity of the community.[17]

The metaphor of the religious field is not intended to suggest that Chinese religion is merely a game; instead, it highlights certain aspects of the dynamics of Chinese religious life:

1. There are rules of play.

   These are established by cultural patterns and values, and encoded in laws and social customs, which are enforced by the government and the local elites.

2. The field is marked by obstacles which must be negotiated.

   Chinese cultural practices as well as social and economic forces shape the needs of the populace, and the ways in which religion can function.

3. There are traditional sets of moves or plays.

   The Chinese religious field contains a common pool of elements which are adapted by various religious groups; the pool can be extended through variation or acceptable forms of innovation.

4. There are at least two sets of players:
- Religious leaders and institutions vie for patronage, devotees, and religious or cultural influence.
- Religious persons and families vie for blessings or boons (health,

wealth, and progeny are perennial favorites), social status or influence, and spiritual fulfillment.

Religious persons must learn not only to negotiate the path, but
also to discern the appropriate goals and means to achieve them.
Since the various temples offer not only transcendent, ultimate goals
but also worldly boons and blessings as proof of the spiritual efficacy
of their deities and practices, players have both short- and long-term
goals in negotiating the course of the religious field.

I developed the notion of religious field to help me understand how
various practices or groups complemented each other within the
wholistic social fabric. It highlights the dynamics of religious activity
on that common ground. I will invoke it often throughout the book to
help the reader visualize the dynamics of religious diversity in China.

Now let us turn to the tale of the accommodation of Buddhism to
Chinese culture to illustrate the dynamics of the Chinese religious field
within the web of patronage, politics, and power.

Pluralism in the Chinese Religious Field:
The Assimilation of Buddhism

When, as a pilgrim, I encountered the story of the introduction and
assimilation of Buddhism into China, beginning in the early centuries
C.E., I began to appreciate the complex real-life dynamics of Chinese
religious inclusivity. Buddhism was a very foreign religion; the challenges facing its entry into China were daunting. The Indian sub-conti-
nent had produced a rich culture, a sophisticated philosophical
heritage, and institutions based on distinctive cultural patterns; China
had also produced a rich literature and sophisticated culture based on
very different patterns. These two cultures had radically different cosmological views, conceptions of time and space, and attitudes toward
the oral and written word. The Buddhists started from a position well
outside of all of the boundaries of the Chinese religious field. Neither
in accord with Chinese values nor recognized by Chinese law,
Buddhism had not entered the gate of the religious field. Moreover, it
represented non-Chinese ("barbarous") beliefs and values, and thus
posed the threat of heresy to its followers.

Both distance and geography (the Himalayas, vast deserts and
steppes roamed by various tribal peoples, and treacherous seas) had
separated these two seats of ancient culture and kept contacts to a
minimum. Thus translation of Buddhist teachings from Sanskrit to
Chinese was a formidable challenge, not merely because of the considerable philosophical differences, but also on purely linguistic grounds.
There was no pool of persons adept in both languages. Because there
were no ready-made cultural categories adequate to express Buddhist

views, early Chinese Buddhist texts made lavish use of Taoist vocabulary. It was the closest match in Chinese culture, but it added an exaggerated Taoistic coloration to the Buddhist teachings. As a result, from the Later Han (23-202 C.E.) through the T'ang (618-907) dynasties, Buddhist and Taoist discourses met and melded into each other. If this meant that the Chinese at first saw Buddhism through a distinctively Taoistic lens, it was equally true that the injection of Buddhist ideas and practices dramatically affected the course of Taoist metaphysical speculation and opened hitherto unforeseen vistas of Taoist philosophy. The Buddhists profited from this translation strategy, because Buddhist deities, ideas, and practices gained currency in *Chinese* terms, thus finding their way onto the local religious fields; they began to blend with local customs and local cults. The Taoists benefited by having their pantheons, myths, rituals, and practices enriched by the store of Buddhist teachings and practices; they adapted these Buddhist enrichments to strengthen their own positions and moves on the Chinese religious field. Over centuries, Buddhists and Taoists borrowed liberally from each other's ritual and meditation techniques, adapting them to their own distinctive terms and practices. The introduction of Buddhism dramatically broadened the range and depth of Taoist thought and practice, and the Buddhist route through Taoistic terminology and religious sensibilities laid the groundwork for the adaptation of Buddhism into distinctively East Asian cults.[18]

Religious borrowing helped Buddhists establish footholds in the local religious fields throughout China. Buddhists also faced a major challenge in accommodating themselves to the Chinese values which the state was committed to uphold. Early Buddhist missionaries felt keenly the Chinese resistance to a religion which did not seem to uphold these traditional values; an early apologist for Buddhism sought to answer the various cultural objections to Buddhist teachings, asserting (as his translators point out) "that it is possible to be a good Chinese and a good Buddhist at the same time, that there is no fundamental conflict between the two ways of life, and that the great truths preached by Buddhism are preached, if in somewhat different language, by Confucianism and Taoism as well."[19]

The Buddhists went well beyond apologetics, adapting themselves centrally to Chinese religious life by offering themselves as religious functionaries for funeral and memorial services. No cultural values were more distinctively Chinese than the obligation to continue the family line through the birth of sons and to venerate the souls of the ancestors. The Chinese initially saw Buddhism as in conflict with these sacred familial duties: 1) because the highest path of Buddhism was leaving one's family to join a religious community, a practice which the Chinese initially saw as in conflict with their strong obligation to continue the family line; and 2) because a core teaching of

Buddhism is that there is no soul, no eternal substratum of the True Self, which seemed to argue against the veneration of ancestors. By establishing themselves as specialists in memorial services, the Buddhists not only found a way to cultivate the support and faith of the Chinese *through their commitment to Chinese family values*, but also succeeded in allaying the fear that Buddhism was un-Chinese.[20] The Buddhist adaptation to Chinese family values required some fancy theological footwork—the Buddhists had to justify commemorating the souls of ancestors who, according to Buddhist theology, had no souls—but it was worth it. By establishing their role in the memorial and funerary rites, the Buddhists purposefully insinuated themselves into an active and advantageous position on the Chinese religious field, where they worked to assimilate local deities and practices to make Buddhism ever more Chinese.

Chinese Buddhist monks naturally stressed passages in traditional Buddhist scriptures which taught filial respect for ancestors:

> We should be filial, obedient, and compassionate toward our parents, our brothers, and other relatives.
> If we are children of the Buddha, we should constantly entertain the earnest wish of being filial and obedient to our parents, teachers, monks, and the Three Jewels [of Buddhist practice].[21]

Moreover, the monk Yüan-chien wrote a Buddhist paean to twenty-four models of filial love.

> Filial heart is the true bodhisattva,
> Filial conduct is the great arena of the *Tao*.
> Filial conduct is the sun or moon shining on a dark street,
> Filial heart is the ship crossing over the sea of misery. . . .
> In Buddhism, piety is the basis for becoming the Buddha,
> In all matters, one must be filial toward one's parents.
> By being in accord with piety in our present life, we can avoid
>   rebirth in the future.
> Filial piety can dissolve all the calamities of life.
> If we practice filial piety toward our aged parents,
> This is the equivalent of opening (and reading) the sutras all
>   day. . . .
> If we wish to emulate the upright characteristics of the Buddha, then there is nothing that can surpass filial piety.[22]

Until the Buddhist persecutions of the ninth century C.E., the traditional Indian Buddhist sects flourished in China, establishing vast centers of Buddhist learning. However, these traditional centers and sects were virtually destroyed in the mid-ninth century during a great persecution of Buddhism, in which thousands of monks, priests, and nuns were defrocked, temples razed, and images melted. This would seem to belie the image of openness and tolerance in the Chinese religious field. However, the persecution was not designed to wipe out Buddhism as a religion or to force conversion to other faiths; rather it curbed the *economic* power of certain schools of Buddhism which had not been fully successful at accommodating to the Chinese religious field.

In the polemical literature of the T'ang dynasty there was, to be sure, an intensification of anti-Buddhist polemic. And yet this polemic was not against Buddhist doctrine as such, but rather against its foreignness, its inadequate assimilation into the Chinese religious field. Han Yü (786-824), an uncompromising public official and trenchant satirist, delivered the most scathing attack on Buddhism in a famous memorial criticizing the emperor's decision to permit a procession of a famous Buddhist relic (the finger bone of the Buddha) in the Chinese capital.

> Now Buddha was a man of the barbarians who did not speak the language of China and wore clothes of a different fashion. . . . If he were still alive today and came to our court by order of his ruler, Your Majesty might condescend to receive him, but it would amount to no more than one audience . . . and he would then be escorted to the borders of the nation, dismissed, and not allowed to delude the masses. How then, when he has long been dead, could his rotten bones, the foul and unlucky remains of his body, be rightly admitted to the palace? Confucius said: "Respect ghosts and spirits, but keep them at a distance!" So when the princes of ancient times went to pay their condolences at a funeral within the state, they sent exorcists in advance with peach wands to drive out evil, and only then would they advance. Now without reason Your Majesty has caused this loathsome thing to be brought in and would personally go to view it. No exorcists have been sent ahead, no peach wands employed.[23]

There are three noteworthy motifs in Han Yü's rhetoric: 1) the Buddha is a mere barbarian (read, foreigner) and should be treated as such; 2) these are the rotten remains of a corpse, and thus inauspicious (no concession to their status as a sacred relic); 3) if they were to be received, it should be with traditional Chinese funerary rituals (the exorcists with the peach wands), thus following the customs of the Chinese religious field. Han Yü's rhetoric reflects the distaste of some Chinese scholars for the residual foreignness of Buddhism. It was attitudes such as Han Yü's that Yüan-chien's Buddhist paean on filial piety sought to counter. Han Yü's essay demonstrates that Buddhism had its ideological enemies, but the persecution of Buddhism was motivated primarily by politics, not by ideology.

The government acted because Buddhism had become too *economically* powerful, threatening the revenue base of the imperial state. Wealthy families had built lavish temples and donated their lands for the support of temples as a form of tax shelter with accompanying religious merit. To make matters worse (from the government's standpoint), monks and nuns were exempt from the tax registers. Thus each son or daughter sent into monastery or convent was removed from the tax rolls as well as from the labor pool.[24] The government became increasingly alarmed at its shrinking tax base and the removal of young men from the labor pool. Emperor Wu-tsung issued an edict in 845:

> Each day finds its monks and followers growing more numerous and its temples more lofty. It wears out the strength of the people with constructions of earth and wood, pilfers their wealth for ornaments of gold and precious objects, causes men to abandon their lords and parents for the company of teachers, and severs man and wife with its monastic decrees. In destroying law and injuring mankind indeed nothing surpasses this doctrine! Now if even one man fails to work the fields, someone must go hungry; if one woman does not tend her silkworms, someone will go cold. At present there are an inestimable number of monks and nuns in the empire, each of them waiting for the farmers to feed him and the silkworms to clothe him, while the public temples and private chapels have reached boundless numbers, all with soaring towers and elegant ornamentation sufficient to outshine the imperial palace itself.[25]

The last line may be said to hold the key: not only had the wealth of Buddhist establishments threatened the tax base; it also threatened to overshadow the imperial palace and its monuments and thus had become in effect a seditious force. The vast Buddhist temples had become overly strong players in the Chinese religious field and were threatening the power of the state to control them.

The persecution of Buddhism, while it destroyed many wonderful temples and works of art, did not wipe out the practice of Buddhism. The most successfully assimilated forms of Buddhism (various forms of Ch'an and Pure Land Buddhism) re-absorbed many aspects of broader Buddhist teachings and practice, creating popular Buddhist movements which continue to this day. The persecution of Buddhism shifted dominance away from Indian-based schools of Buddhism to the forms which had arisen in China, and thus were the most fully assimilated.

The story of the entry, assimilation, persecution, and survival of Buddhism in China is a revealing illustration of how a foreign teaching might fare in the Chinese religious field. The Buddhists had to acquaint themselves with the common pool of religious elements so that they could play on the Chinese religious field. They had to accommodate to basic Chinese values, particularly family values. They had to learn the rules of the game both in dealing with governmental authorities and in attracting patrons and devotees. They had to identify a distinctive role or position (funerary rites) which would give them a strong niche, overcoming their outsider status. They learned that on this field a player can be too successful, and can thus lose his/her place; it was, ironically, the economic success of the great Buddhist cults that was ultimately their downfall.

The Buddhist players who accommodated most fully to the rules of the Chinese religious field (Ch'an and Pure Land) established strong and lasting positions. It was they who borrowed most extensively from the common pool of deities and practices, who emulated native genres of writing, and who cast Buddhist teachings in the practical this-worldly vein so attractive to the Chinese. It was they who made Buddhism genuinely accessible to the Chinese people.

A striking aspect of this tale is the long, slow process of Buddhist assimilation. It was nearly a millennium before the process of identifying the enduring forms of Chinese Buddhism was complete. The moral of the tale is that playing on the Chinese religious field is a complex and subtle art. The Buddhists were successful in gaining access and finding a foothold, but it took them many centuries to establish themselves securely in the hearts of the Chinese.

Final Thoughts

The tale of assimilation of Chinese Buddhism was of immense value to me as a pilgrim in Chinese culture, for it helped me to understand the real-life, on-the-ground dynamics of religious diversity. It spoke eloquently of cultural resistance to foreign religious values and patterns, and how these must be patiently interpreted and accommodated for any mutual understanding to emerge. Thus I came to see that my pilgrimage would be a long one, and that patience and persistence would be required of me if I were to make progress in genuine interfaith understanding.

It exposed the many dimensions of potential religious misunderstandings (linguistic, familial, political, economic, customary). Every religious tradition is embedded in a nest of cultural patterns, each one of which must be integrated into a new cultural setting. Under-standing another religion would require focus on more than religion by itself; it demanded an understanding of the embeddedness of reli-gion, of what was at stake on many levels in each belief or practice.

It illustrated the ingenious adaptations which religious groups make as they adapt to new cultural settings. Presumably such adapta-tions are also required of Christianity, not only as it enters cultures originally dominated by other religions, but also as it adapts to the new global religious pluralism in what have been seen as Christian cultures.

Most of all, it exposed (by contrast) the marked impatience of North Americans to have changes effected and issues settled within a remarkably brief time frame. Granting that post-modern culture moves at lightning speed compared to traditional Chinese culture, nonetheless we as Americans profoundly underestimate the complexi-ty and overestimate the pace of cultural change.

The conceptual model of the Chinese religious field helped me to make sense of this tale and to visualize its dynamics. This heuristic model will also help illuminate other tales to be related in the follow-ing chapters.

CHAPTER 5

Cultural Unity and Local Variation

Vying for Control on the Chinese Religious Field

The Sages of the Three Teachings are heroes who stand firmly on earth and reach to heaven. Clearly there is no room for differences. Therefore it is said, "There are not two Ways under heaven; the sage or worthy does not have two minds."

—Hsün Tzu

Our eminent Founder [the first Ming emperor] united the world and established the domain. He respected Confucius, Lao Tzu, and Sâkyamuni [Buddha] as though they were one person. Therefore in the Collection of Imperial Writings, *he often speaks of the Sages of the Three Teachings. And he often uses these two statements [i.e., the above two-part quotation] to judge them in order to show that they are not different. Now the Way is identical with the mind, so how can there be any differences? Not even ignorant men and women, not even insects and plants, go outside the purview of this Way and this mind. How much less the Sages of the Three Teachings? Even if one wished to have two Ways or two minds, one would not be able to do so.*

—Li Chih
San-chiao p'in

"King"

The character for king symbolized, in ancient Chinese thought, the role of the ruler (represented by the vertical line) to hold in harmony the realms of heaven, the human, and the earth (the three horizontal lines from top to bottom).

The model of the Chinese religious field was a major breakthrough in my pilgrimage. I now had a useful tool for understanding the examples of Chinese religious life which I encountered, so that I could move ahead with more confidence and less trepidation. The tale of the assimilation of Chinese Buddhism brought me to a higher plateau, for I had begun to face the real-life embeddedness of religious life and practice; I had left behind my romantic and overly idealistic portrait of Chinese inclusivism. The Chinese had not transcended all competitive tendencies or power struggles; they had simply developed a different set of strategies, strategies that evaded the ills of religious exclusivism. Having climbed to this plateau and accustomed myself to the elevation, I was now ready to confront more directly the issues of power and competition. Who controlled (or vied for control of) the Chinese religious field? What was at stake for the various competing parties? How did competition and control play themselves out?

As I continued my journey with questions of power in the forefront, I found myself facing another challenge to understanding. I noticed striking discrepancies between the portraits of Chinese religious life portrayed by the normative texts, particularly those endorsed by the imperial government and its representatives, and reports on Chinese belief and practice based on the field reports of anthropologists. In the 1970s, while I was in graduate school, scholars trained in textual work were just beginning to read anthropological reports seriously, and anthropologists were reading (and challenging) work based solely on texts. This occurred both because Chinese studies as a whole was flourishing, producing a stream of provocative and important scholarship; and also because, with the development of social history, the study of Taoism and vernacular literature, and the opening of research on sub-elites and local elites, the vast territory between the normative texts and field reports was being entered by many, including this pilgrim. Both textual and field-work based models for understanding Chinese society were gaining nuances as our knowledge of Chinese history and culture grew. The issues of power had to be viewed in two directions: from the top down, and from the bottom up. In this chapter, I first discuss the origins and implications of the Chinese myth of cosmological unity and its implications for the religious field. I then explore the motivations of the imperial government in embracing, celebrating, and controlling religion. Turning to the bottom-up view, I explore the room for local variation or dissent within the unity of Chinese culture. I conclude with the tale of Ching-ming Tao (Way of the Pure and Perspicacious) to illustrate the interplay of the unifying and local forces in the Chinese religious field.

In the last chapter, I recounted the tale of the slow assimilation of Buddhism to Chinese culture through its accommodation to mainstream Chinese values of filial piety and ancestor veneration. The foreign Buddhists gained entree to the Chinese religious field by aligning themselves with the values and practices of Chinese law and custom. As a foreign pilgrim in Chinese culture, I too was acutely aware of my outsider status, of the many cultural patterns and codes I would have to master to enter this amazing world. The Chinese have a long-standing and proud sense of their civilization, encoded in practice, recorded in the classics, interpreted by the literate elite, and enforced by the imperial government. Outsiders had to bow to the values which represented this civilization before they could enter the gate of the Chinese religious field.

The Chinese imperial government, supported by the scholarly elite, sustained the sense of values and of Chinese cultural unity. In the epigraph to this chapter, Neo-Confucian writer Li Chih (1527-1602) praised the Ming dynasty founder T'ai-tsu (r. 1368-1398) for uniting the realm both politically and religiously; T'ai-tsu accomplished this by respecting "Confucius, Lao Tzu, and Sâkyamuni [Buddha] as though they were one person." T'ai-tsu, in other words, understood that political unity, cultural unity, and religious unity were of a piece, and that his role as emperor was to sustain unity on all three levels. As Li Chih remarked, if even plants and insects are included in the Way, how could any of the Three Teachings stand outside its purview? The unity of the cosmos was the foundation and base for the unity of civilization and of religion.

The State and the Myth[1] of Cultural Unity

The distinctive relation of the state to religion was shaped by the early history of China.

The Ancient System of Priestly Governance

From the beginnings of Chinese civilization, earthly rule was founded on Heavenly authority; the ruler was also a priest. The rulers regularly consulted Heaven by means of prayer and divination, seeking counsel for everything from hunts to auspicious days for government ceremonies.[2] The ruler's priestly role, his connection to the ancestral or autochthonous nature deities in Heaven, gave him the power to rule; he was but the medium for the deities who exercised sovereign authority.

In the period known as the Warring States (403-221 B.C.E.), a number of leaders vied for supremacy in China by means of military and political strategies, directly challenging the traditional power of the ruler as priest. It was a period marked by political intrigue, alliances and counter-alliances, plots, battles, assassinations, and coups. Stronger states conquered, absorbed, or dominated weaker neighbors. China was moving toward unification by force, and the issue was only which state would survive the struggle.

The period of the Warring States precipitated a *religious* crisis for ancient Chinese culture, for the premise that the authority of the ruler, of government itself, rested on divine guidance of the gods and ancestors was now challenged. Antireligious positions asserted that strong laws and effective statecraft were the true basis of sovereign authority. This challenge stimulated traditionalists to reinterpret and elaborate ancient models of ancestor and nature worship as alternatives to the antireligious position; these elaborations became the cores of the Confucian and Taoist traditions. Thus an intense socio-political struggle laid the intellectual foundations of the Chinese religious field. In this formative period of Chinese history, religious thought was deeply enmeshed in brutal worldly issues.

The victor among the Warring States was the Ch'in dynasty (221-209 B.C.E.), the champion of the most secular of all the contending ideologies, that of the "statecrafters." The statecrafters scoffed at the ancient beliefs that sovereignty was morally and ritually grounded in Heaven, as much sacerdotal as it was political. The statecrafters advocated authoritarian government, sustained by strict laws, military power, and efficient governmental institutions. The Ch'in dynasty, in its brief reign of twelve years, accomplished a great deal toward building a unified state, but it also imposed a strict police state, ruthlessly destroying all writings which opposed its official views. The strain of massive public works and political repression took its toll on the people and eroded their support of the government. The Ch'in dynasty fell at the death of its first ruler, and became the "evil empire" of traditional Chinese historiography.

Some of the achievements of the Ch'in were highly beneficial, but traditional historiography gave most of the credit for creating the unified culture of China to the successor Han dynasty (206 B.C.E. - 202 C.E.). The Han built on the positive efforts at centralization while developing an ideology and cosmological/religious foundation for cultural unity that became definitive for the remaining two millennia of Chinese imperial history.

The Han System of Cultural Unity

According to Han ideology, the Chinese ruler was the pivot which held in harmony and balance the three tiers of cosmology[3]: the heavens, the earth, and the human realm. This image or metaphor is built on the visual form of the character for ruler (*wang*) (see figure 5.1). The ideogram has three horizontal lines, representing heaven, earth, and the human, with a single vertical stroke in the center as

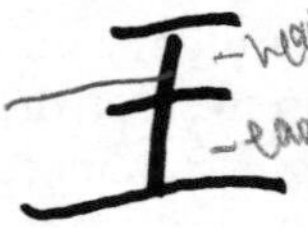

Figure 5.1

the connecting link; the vertical stroke represents the ruler, who connects the three tiers.[4] How were these three tiers held in balance? Cosmological balance was sutained by the ruler through acts of governance, moral propriety, observance of ritual duties, and divination. Thus the Han thinkers transformed and expanded ancient motifs of the ruler's priestly duties in the service of a unified imperial state.

In order for the new religious ideology to become effective, the Han thinkers also had to reconcile the cosmological systems and religious practices which had previously developed in the various states. The Han government gathered and correlated diverse cosmological principles of the various religious specialists into a single system, based on an elaborate series of *correspondences*.[5] Having learned its lesson from the resistance to strict laws and ruthless enforcement which had led to the fall of the Ch'in, the Han did not impose only one out of the many competing options; instead it created an ingenious *overarching system* which could accommodate already existing systems through a system of correspondences. By intentionally combining many systems, the Han thinkers established a central feature of the relatively inclusive Chinese religious field: a mechanism to accommodate local practices into a religious system which expressed China's cultural unity, and thus sustained the sovereign authority of the imperial state. This move completed the unification of many feudal states, for it gave the unity a cultural basis and an integrating mechanism.

The success of this system and the ideology which surrounded it was remarkable. From the Han dynasty onward the Chinese had an unshakable belief in the *normative unity* of Chinese culture; Chinese civilization was to embrace all under heaven (*T'ien-hsia*). Although China was often politically divided into two or more states, and although premodern communications systems made the whole of China nearly impossible to govern from one center, the Chinese elite steadfastly maintained that cosmological, cultural, and political unity were normative. The three levels of unity could not be disentangled. The role of China's ruler was to unite and harmonize the entire cosmos— the civilized world. The religious field was also structured to embrace "all under Heaven," as Li Chih insisted in the epigraph to this chapter. That such an ideology would last over two millennia and be adopted by foreign rulers of China such as Mongols, Jurchens, and Manchus, is testimony to the power of the cultural system and its religious underpinnings.

Official Patronage as a Strategy for Affirming and Controlling Multiplicity

We noted above that the Chinese cosmological system was developed in large part so that the government could extend its mantle over the

王

whole of the Chinese civilized world. For two thousand years of imperial history, the Chinese state cult retained a significant ritual role for
the ruler, symbolizing his (very rarely, her) role in unifying and maintaining the cosmos. This ritual role also extended to the obligation of
the ruler and governmental officials at all levels to provide patronage
and official guidance for religion in the realm. As noted in chapter 4,
the Chinese state reserved to itself the authority to establish the appropriate bounds of religious belief, writing, and practice; there was no
notion of separation of church and state. From the T'ang dynasty (618-
907) onward, the government sought to make official patronage of
religion at least as powerful as the patronage of local families and
notables; in other words, it sought to extend the imperial government's
role in the sponsorship (and control) of religion.[6]

Government Mechanisms for Control of Religion

In the T'ang dynasty, the government established imperial bureaus of
Buddhism and Taoism and sponsored bibliographic projects to publish great compendia of Confucian, Taoist, and Buddhist writings, as
well as encyclopedias on history and other matters. The state bureaus
kept records, published books, and administered government regula-
tions about the classifications of priests, books, and rituals.[7] There
were no state bureaus for folk religion, so that any imperially recorded
and approved religious item had to be classified as Buddhist, Taoist, or
Confucian.[8]

The T'ang government also developed and controlled the state
examination system to award Confucian degrees, which qualified can-
didates for government service.[9] The state established an official Confucian cult, building temples to honor Confucian worthies in seats of
government throughout the realm, and officially bestowing the title of
"worthy" on selected persons.

The government's management of the Chinese religious world was
exercised both through legal control (including persecution) and
through patronage. Government laws and edicts outlawed various
sects and groups, prohibited specific religious practices, burned texts
as heretical, and banned public assemblies.[10] The motive was two-fold:
1) to maintain the value base of Chinese culture, and 2) to ensure that
religion continued to support rather than threaten the status quo.

In late imperial China (fifteenth century-1912), the status quo was
fragile, threatened by external and internal forces. In this period, the
government tended to see any large-scale popular activity as a threat.
Modern scholars have studied "folk Buddhist" (millenarian or White
Lotus) groups, which arose sometime around the twelfth century and
became a powerful cultural phenomenon in the fifteenth century. The

government at times saw folk Buddhist movements as potentially or actually seditious (and hence heretical, in legal terms), although the research suggests that neither the beliefs nor the practices were intended to be seditious or threatening.[11] These folk Buddhist sects were carefully watched and sometimes vigorously persecuted by the state. Some of these groups hastened to accommodate their writings more carefully to mainstream religious ideas, thereby protecting themselves against suspicion.

Government Patronage

Although a major motivation of the government was control, its sponsorship and patronage of religious practices also condoned a broad pattern of religious multiplicity. Each county seat not only had its official academy and Confucian hall of worthies, but also had a number of imperially sponsored temples, labeled as Buddhist or Taoist. These official temples were listed in county and prefectural gazetteers, along with tidbits of their history and their official and imperial patronage. Government sponsorship authorized the tonsure of monks and nuns, and provided stipends in support of the temples. Local officials were expected to attend major rituals at the official temples as representatives of the government; their presence as a representative of the emperor replicated locally the ritual role of the emperor at the capital. The officials paid respects to the deities on behalf of the state and asked for the support of the deities in maintaining order, thus sustaining the harmony of the cosmos.

The government also asserted its patronage and control of local religion by appointing (i.e., giving a title to) the deity of the city wall temple (*ch'eng-huang miao*). Generally a local hero around whom stories of religious protection had posthumously collected, the city wall deity became a spirit general with an assignment to protect the city and its surrounding countryside.[12] In appointing the city-wall gods, the government paid public homage to a local hero and coopted his powers into a heavenly hierarchy which sustained the unity of the empire. The government embraced all significant religious communities so that they would form part of the religious support of imperial power and order. I will recount one such instance in the tale which ends this chapter.

Unity and Diversity: Strategies Which Leave Room for Variation

The paternalistic controlling impulse of the government was only one side of the dynamic of the Chinese religious field. China is a vast coun-

王

try, geographically larger and embracing more languages and dialects than Europe, a patchwork quilt comprised of many subcultures and minority peoples who have lived under the cultural and political dominance of "Han" (Chinese) culture.

Because of the striking diversities among regions and linguistic groups, local communities had to exercise considerable ingenuity to mask from themselves and from the authorities in the capital the extent of their deviation from the standard norm, as defined in law and in the governmentally sanctioned classics. For some years scholars who read both studies based on official documents and the work of anthropologists in regions far from the capital marveled at the discrepancies between these two pictures of Chinese religious life.

The Chinese empire, at least by the time of the T'ang dynasty (618-907), was vast and diverse. Lacking modern communications, there was no way for the central government to be fully informed about activities in the provinces, nor could it fully control them. This was not for lack of interest, but rather a reflection of the limitations of central control over vast areas in the premodern world.

This section deals with the role of regional dialect and local moral consensus in allowing some room for variation within standard orthodoxy. This space for variation affords freedom for varieties in both the rules and style of play in local or regional versions of the Chinese religious field.

The Chinese Language as a Vehicle for Expressing Diversity

Chinese culture is a patchwork of subcultures, dialect groups, and minority peoples, and the myth of cultural unity is to some degree a myth in both senses of the word: a mistaken assertion, and an attempt to create reality by representing it as a story invested with meaning which can be sustained through ritual practice. One of the primary bonds sustaining the unity of Chinese culture was its written language, a *lingua franca* for the educated elite which could be read in a variety of diverse spoken dialects.

Chinese is not an alphabetical language. That is, there is not a limited number of letters or symbols representing the sounds of the spoken language, which can then be transcribed into writing. Rather it is an ideographic language, with tens of thousands of characters or ideograms developed to represent individual words. Some of the characters started as a pictograph or ideogram, a representation of the thing to which the spoken word referred. The pictorial hint worked as a mnemonic device, helping the reader to recognize the word indicated. Many words, however, could not be easily pictured, and so a character was built by combining a classifier (indicating the kind of thing it

| Figure 5.2 | Figure 5.3 |

is) with a homophonic picture. Thus the word for horse (*ma*) was originally a picture of a horse, but combined with the classifier for "woman," it became mother (*ma*); with the classifier for "mouth," it became a question indicator (*ma?*); with the classifier for "blood," it became a curse (*ma*) (see figure 5.2). Or, horse can itself be a classifier to indicate "horsy things" so that with the phonic *ch'i*, it means to gallop (see figure 5.3). Other markers were added to other characters until a vast vocabulary had been built up.[13]

The characters did give some indication of a sound, but could not be read easily, since the phonic element was both hard to identify and might have evolved over time; the pronunciation of each character had to be memorized individually.

While Chinese is not the easiest language to learn to read and write, the writing system has one aspect of genius for maintaining Chinese cultural unity: speakers of the scores of Chinese dialects could each learn the written language (*wen-yen*), pronouncing it in their own local language. This contrasts sharply with Latin, which served as a *lingua franca* in medieval Europe, and was always and clearly distinct from spoken languages. One could read *wen-yen* in and through the lens of one's mother tongue.[14]

Thus the canonical and normative texts which defined Chinese-ness were in this pan-Chinese written language, which was pronounceable in, but not the same as, the spoken language of the particular region; *wen-yen* could be read by literate persons in their local dialectical pronunciation, but it did not transcribe the local dialect itself. This allowed an opening for two levels of discourse: the more universal, which took place in the written language and followed the norms and mores of a unified Chinese culture, and the local dialect, incomprehensible to outsiders, in which the locals could sustain their linguistic and cultural distinctiveness.

The two-tiered language system also allowed for stories told or written[15] in the local vernacular to reflect regional perceptions of reality, including their distinctive interpretations of the imperial Sacred Edicts.[16] Even novels could reflect a view of the Chinese way which stretched the boundaries and sensibilities of the imperial orthodoxy.[17] The Chinese people and local communities often acceded to the political authority of the imperial government, but reserved to themselves

王

some moral authority based on their own experience. If the local community and the representatives of the imperial government judged
that a practice was normative and supportive of moral values and the
social order, then it was accepted as canonical or orthodox even if it
seemed to clash with what was written in the classics or the legal code.
Thus, a local practice regarding burial or mourning might differ significantly from that prescribed in the classical texts, but as long as the
local practice reflected "the way things are done" the discrepancy was
simply ignored. Barbara Ward has called this ingenious stratagem
"varieties of the conscious model."[18] Outsiders who served as government officials in the district often noted the distinctive local customs,
but if they seemed to reflect cultural normalcy (to reinforce rather
than undercut social order and harmony), this was not seen to be in
conflict with the Chinese Way.

Thus we have seen that although the government sought to control
and co-opt religion, it did so in the spirit of embracing all forms of
religious life which sustained the social order, and hence strengthened
the sovereignty of the state. Local deviations from the norm were tol-
erated, so long as they were, at bottom, establishmentarian. The
Chinese religious field was, with the support of the government officials, both capacious and sufficiently flexible about rules of play to
embrace a broad diversity of religious life and practice.

The specific role of the government in embracing religious diversity
and supporting emergent religious movements can be well illustrated
with the case of Ching-ming Tao.

The Tale of Ching-ming Tao
(Way of the Pure and Perspicacious)

In many periods of Chinese history, emperors realized that the best
way to deal with the variety of local religions and powerful temples
was to embrace them by means of imperial patronage, thereby pulling
them into the orbit of religious support of imperial power. Such temples became official temples and regularly offered prayers and ceremonies for the health of the state, with local magistrates and other
officials in attendance. The temples in turn received financial support,
authorization for more clergy, and funds to hold visible and dignified
ritual ceremonies which might attract the patronage of local gentry
families.

Once a temple became a major Buddhist or Taoist monastery
(which trained and housed ordained priests or monks), official recognition was more or less assured; in such cases recognition followed
upon success. The more complex and fascinating story, however, is
how a local religious group functioning outside of the bounds of either

Buddhism or Taoism, came to be enfolded into the system of imperial patronage during the Sung dynasty (960-1279). This tale shows both government authorities and local believers maximizing their positions on the religious field.

What came to be known as Ching-ming Tao was originally a local popular religion, founded by Wu Meng (flourished, third century, C.E.). Wu Meng performed magic, exorcised demons and monsters, and taught some rudimentary forms of ritual and self-cultivation from the common Chinese religious field.[19] Between 644 and 670, Hsü Sun (239-292), who had originally been Wu Meng's disciple, came to be venerated as the primary deity of the movement. Devotion to Hsü Sun was well established at the group's center on Hsi-shan, and shrines to him appeared all over southeast China from the Sung dynasty onward.

Hsü Sun was lionized as a local magistrate who used religious arts to battle demons, monsters, and plagues. Over the centuries he also developed a reputation as a deity who helped besieged communities defend themselves against bandits. His effectiveness as a protector positioned his religious movement as a defender of the state, and thus attracted elite patronage.[20]

Sung imperial interest in the cult began when early Sung emperors adapted a divination system devised by Hsü Sun, which had reportedly been very helpful to the Sui Emperor Yang-ti (r. 605-616). Sung emperor Chen-tsung (r. 998-1022) named Hsü's temple Yü-lung kuan (The Abbey of Jade Beneficence).

Sung imperial patronage entered a new phase under emperor Hui-tsung (r. 1102-1125). Hui-tsung once fell asleep reading and dreamed he saw a Taoist master holding a cup decorated with a nine-flower pattern, attended by two men dressed as priests and holding swords. The Taoist master informed the emperor that he was Hsü Sun, an official in Heaven, whom the gods had dispatched to aid the Sung government in its present difficulties with the Jurchen.[21] Hsü reported that during his tenure as a magistrate in the third century, he had defeated demons and malicious spiritual forces (*yao-ch'i*) in his domain. Since the incursion of barbarian forces once again threatened the region he had once governed, he was coming to the aid of the throne.[22] This account of spiritual prowess caught Hui-tsung's interest, for the emperor sought help in warding off the threats of the Jurchen invaders and in controlling monsters and demons, whose worship he believed threatened the stability of the Chinese religious field.

On waking from his dream, the emperor ordered his attendants to locate Hsü Sun's temple.[23] He had a portrait painted from his description of the deity in his dream. This portrait he circulated to temples throughout the land, asking them if this deity resided in their temple. The circulation of the portrait gave local temple leaders a chance to promote their causes. When the temple had been located, the emperor

王

sent a young Taoist to convey his respects to the deity Hsü Sun. In 1112, Hui-tsung sent jade tablets to announce his patronage of the temple and ordered an elaborate seven-day *chiao* ritual with thirty-seven Taoist masters and ritual masters in attendance; the banquet on the last day of ritual fed 360 guests.[24]

A few months later, Hsü Sun once again appeared in Hui-tsung's dreams to thank him for his efforts on his behalf. He lamented that his main temple, Yü-lung kuan, was in a state of disrepair and asked the emperor to restore it. (One wonders if the temple leaders had not made the same case to the imperial envoys who brought the emperor's messages of respect.) The emperor immediately ordered the restoration; he had six major halls and twelve minor halls restored, installed new images, repainted the murals, sent new bronze incense burners, vases, and other ritual equipment, and personally penned couplets and inscriptions for the temple, which credited Hsü Sun with saving the region from a Jurchen invasion.[25]

In 1118 Hui-tsung incorporated this temple into the system of imperially sponsored official temples by naming it a *kung*, an official Taoist temple. Imperial recognition brought with it a new layer of religious duties, representing ritual traditions and practices extraneous to the internal and local history of Ching-ming Tao. Priests would now regularly perform rituals in the service of the state. The religious leaders of Ching-ming Tao would not originally have been trained in such elaborate rituals.[26] Imperial rituals, such as the *chiao*, required the temporary or permanent assignment to the temples of formally trained Taoist priests. The assignments of these priests in itself changed the character of the temple, and brought it into the mainstream of imperially recognized forms of religion. This was the price of the considerable benefit of the lavish restoration paid for by the emperor.

The local traditions of the group were not, however, entirely eclipsed by their entry into the mainstream of official temples. The author of Hsü's biography describes in some detail a pilgrimage at the shrine.[27] The pilgrimage path was believed to retrace routes which Hsü had traveled as a magistrate. Each twist and turn of the path, each ford of a river, had a story or tradition connected with Hsü's life—his battle with a white snake, or his conquering of an evil force. The account of the pilgrimage, which is local and popular, suggests that the group maintained its local traditions and practices alongside the new Taoist ones. Thus two levels of ritual, one official and one local, existed side by side. The character and stature of the religious institution had been expanded, but at least during the Sung, the community maintained its local traditions while honoring the official boons and duties of becoming an imperially sponsored temple. Two distinct religious traditions were practiced at the same temple.

工

The story of Ching-ming Tao helps us to understand the role of the government and of local tradition in the Chinese religious field. Imperial patronage and recognition had clear advantages for a religious institution: restoration of temples, financial support, the residence of priests trained for formal and impressive rites, the nearly mandatory participation of local officials and elites in ritual activities designed to support the state. On the other hand, there was room for local tradition and the continuation of some of the older practices alongside the official ritual roles of a recognized temple. The government had its view of the role and responsibilities of the temple; the local adepts had their view of its history, traditions, and practices.

The Chinese religious field supported both the myth of cultural unity and the richness of local variation. The local cult, in order to attract imperial patronage, had to accommodate to the nationally recognized categories for religion; the imperial government, in order to co-opt the support of the local religious movement, had to honor and support the local deity and his temple. Both Ching-ming Tao and the Sung government benefited from their relationship, but each side tacitly acknowledged the discrepancy between local and national perceptions and made room for both local and imperial customs and practices.

Final Thoughts

In my early days as a pilgrim in China, I had a tendency to idealize or romanticize Chinese practices, seeing them as somehow more idealistic and less compromised than the religious history of Christianity. Still a young woman, I shared with many young Christians disillusionment at the imperfections of the Christian churches and the contradictions between ideals and practices. The messy and compromised history of the church, often enmeshed in power struggles within its ranks and with secular authorities, seemed to sully true Christianity.

However, anything beyond the most superficial acquaintance with Chinese religion insists that there is no division between the sacred and secular, between religion and politics: religion is central to society at all levels, and is thus deeply embedded in political, social, and cultural struggles.

It was an important lesson for me to realize that Chinese religious inclusivity did not arise from some transcendent idealism, but rather was embedded in the commitments of both the ruling classes and the local populations to their own religious visions and paths. The Chinese negotiated religious diversity shrewdly, and they allowed space for others in order to ensure their mutual survival and flourishing.

The story of Ching-ming Tao helped me grasp more concretely how

王

the Chinese accommodated the pressures for cultural unity while honoring the local. Different embodiments of this movement could coexist as different parties made room for the other view, while holding to their own.

One the other hand, the role of Taoist priest Pai Yü-ch'an illustrated to me how readily the boundaries between the government version of Ching-ming Tao and the local version could be crossed. Pai was invited to Yü-lung kung to officiate at specialized Taoist rituals, the new rituals required by the recognition of the temple. He stayed on to write a detailed record of Hsü's life and the development of the religious movement. Although Pai came to the temple to represent mainstream Taoist rituals, he was so moved by the religious vitality of the local movement that he left a vivid record of their story and local practices. Pai did not join Ching-ming Tao; his own practice followed another school. Yet he celebrated Ching-ming Tao's contributions to the Chinese religious field. Pai had no personal agenda with regard to Ching-ming Tao. He simply saw both Ching-ming Tao and his own practices as part of the Chinese religious field; he might well cite the saying of Hsün Tzu invoked by Li Chih in the epigraph to this chapter: "There are not two Ways under heaven; the sage or worthy does not have two minds." Pai's celebration of Ching-ming Tao is eloquent testimony to the genuine cultural pattern of religious inclusivity sustained by the Han system of cultural unity.

Pai Yü-ch'an's role as the chronicler of Ching-ming Tao, author of a vibrant account of its history and its spiritual legacy, helped me to discern my role as a scholar of other religions. Pai initially came in a formal priestly capacity on a temporary visit, but stayed on as a guest, accepting the hospitality of the tradition in order to learn about it and to share that knowledge with others. He honored the history and the religious values of the tradition, recording them faithfully in his account along with original sources. As it happened, his work became the most vibrant record of and witness to the religious vitality of this movement; he became, in a sense, an unwitting theologian, or authoritative commentator, of the tradition.

More than twelve years after my original visit to Chinese territory, I found myself in a similar position. I had gone to China to do dissertation research on Lin Chao-en, on whom I would later publish the only full-length book available in any language. In the 1980s, Lin Chao-en's religious movement was being revived in Fukien and southeast China, and I was invited to a conference as the major authority (i.e, essentially a theologian) of the movement. It was a strange sensation.

Like Pai Yü-ch'an, I had sought to honor the integrity of Lin's life and teaching, and to convey in my work the religious vitality of the movement which he founded. Both Pai and I no doubt benefited from our sustained and respectful attention to the values and virtues of the traditions which we chronicled. Yet in neither of our cases did this mean a conversion or even a dramatic change of direction in our own spiritual developments and affiliation. We were both honoring religious communities whose teachings deserved broader attention, and seeking to discern and learn from virtues and values which might enrich our own lives and those of our communities.

Too often scholars of religion have claimed to be only "learning about" or "teaching about" the religions they study; that is disingenuous, since it ignores the ways in which all genuine learning enriches the self and contributes to growth. On the other hand, too many Christians have assumed that all exposure to another religion in effect opens one to the competition and weakens one's loyalty to one's own community. Such an attitude is overly defensive, and it overlooks the fact that a religious person may be well positioned to appreciate the religious values and qualities of other religious persons' lives, enhancing one's own religious sensibilities in the process. The middle ground is to be a respectful guest, to honor another tradition as far as possible on its own terms, and to be open to benefiting from the exchange, while at the same time being clear about who I am and how my identity and location shape my experience as a learner of the other tradition. If I can do both of those, I will be able to learn well and also recount what I have learned effectively to those in my own community.

CHAPTER **6**

Myriad Spirits and the Transcendent in the Religious Field

[Liu Yi-chih (1078-1160)] said, "The sentient beings are the essence of things (t'i-pen) and the fulfillment of enlightenment (yüan-ch'eng). So we and the bodhisattva [Kuan-yin] are the same, and there is no difference between us and her. Because of this non-duality (wu-erh) and non-differentiation (wu-pieh), the faith in the hearts of the sentient beings extends everywhere without physical trace. The bodhisattva not only has no fixed identity but also no fixed dwelling. Yet, you put up a statue in a designated place for them to seek refuge. Are you not creating a false distinction?"

Chiu replied, "Not so. The goddess's manifestations are limitless. Because she has no one place of her own, but is worshipped in the hearts of believers, she thus has a place. I see that monks and lay people go in front of the statue, gather their robes and bow, burn incense and pray on their knees, and tell her of all their illnesses and troubles, and ask for help. Full of sincere emotion, sweat dripping down their faces, they tell her their inner thoughts. The bodhisattva responded to their faith by appearing in a dream.

"Ultimately, they [the bodhisattva and sentient beings] are as one. I admire the place she is worshipped and make it imposing in order to augment their faith. If they believe, in one instant they view matter, and they understand emptiness. Then they will attain enlightenment. They will know that the

---

"Many Spirits, One Way"
These characters represent the Chinese affirmation of both a plethora of deities and the transcendent unity of the Tao.

> bodhisattva does not arise from her image. She is everywhere,
> in all directions. Every place is her place of worship. And this
> place of worship is nowhere specific."
> —Liu Yi-chih
> *temple inscription from* T'iao-hsi chi

萬
神
一
道

By this point in my journey, I was well on the way to developing powers for apprehending the dynamics of the Chinese religious field. I had confronted the role of power and patronage, of political motivations both at the national and local levels. I had begun to appreciate the interplay between the myth of cultural unity and the realities of local variation, as government authorities and local communities vied to promote their interests in controlling a religious place or tradition. However, more challenges were ahead for this pilgrim.

My next challenge was to deal with the stunning and vast array of gods worshipped by the Chinese. I began to wonder how such rich diversity could maintain any unity whatsoever—wasn't this simply a case of "anything goes"? How did the tens of thousands of gods and spirits relate to the Way of Heaven which encompassed all in the Chinese religious field? Did the many competing deities offering worldly boons suggest, as early Western observers tended to believe, that Chinese religion was merely pragmatic and this-worldly and had no impulse toward the transcendent?

The temple inscription of Liu Yi-chih, which formed the epigraph to this chapter, raised a related question: if the Bodhisattva Kuan-yin was omnipresent and could take many forms, how did one justify building a statue, which occupied only one place and only one form of the bodhisattva, for her worship?

In this chapter I deal with the issues surrounding this relationship of the multiplicity of deities and images to the transcendent unity of the Way. In it, I explore: the relationship of deities to their images, the importance of a deity's demonstration of power to sustain worship (and vice versa), the multiplicity of spirits in any local religious field, the moral continuum of humans and spirits, and the theology of transcendence. I conclude with a tale of how a single Taoist religious ritual simultaneously honored the transcendental aspects of the holy and the particularistic worldly or popular expressions.

The Relations of Gods to Their Images

A foreign visitor to a Chinese temple or shrine is immediately struck by the plethora of images: crude and elaborate, small and large. Some are little more than carved dolls; others are larger than life-size, decorated with gilt, paint, lacquer, and/or elaborately embroidered garments. Many images boast beards made of human hair. If the temple

萬
神
一
道

is too poor to have a carved image, it may have a drawing, painting, or wood-block print to portray the deity. These deities are offered incense, food and drink, and money; they may be feted with music and dance, or taken in a sedan chair to visit their territory or to attend a rite or festival at another temple. They are approached in prayer by individuals and asked by priests and shamans to lend their power to rituals. There is no question that these images are the focus of piety and worship.[1]

There is a tendency among Christians, particularly Protestants, to assume that such worship involving images or pictures of deities is necessarily idolatry, a confusion of the nontranscendent with the transcendent. There are, however, indications in Chinese ritual practice that this charge of idolatry is misplaced; these images are not confused with the higher spiritual powers which they represent.

There is, for example, the ceremony of opening the eyes, the ritual for installing an image in a Chinese temple. Anyone can purchase an image of a particular deity, but such figures are merely statues until they are ritually invested in a temple (or at a home altar) by means of the *k'ai-yen* (opening the eyes) ceremony.[2] The *k'ai-yen* ritual invites the heavenly deity (of which the statue is a depiction) to descend and inhabit the image with its luminosity (*ling*), thus animating it with spiritual power. In traditional times, the ceremony also included the insertion of paper drawings of organs into an opening in the rear of the statue, vivifying the hollow wooden body with symbolic organs. Only so long as the image was inhabited by the *ling* of the deity was it considered holy.[3] The presence of *ling* meant that the deity inhabited its image and could perform miracles in answer to prayers. If the image was not in good condition, the deity would not have a "healthy body" to inhabit, and its power to perform miracles would be harmed.[4] A natural disaster, such as flood or fire, could injure the *ling* of the image; in that case, the image might either be discarded, replaced with a new image, or ritually revived with another *k'ai-yen* ceremony.

Another practice for revivifying images can be seen in the phenomenon of branch temples of a famous deity, such as Ma Tsu.[5] Such temples are formal branches of an original temple, extending the spiritual grace and prowess of the deity to outlying locations. The branch temples periodically send representatives to the main temple, carrying their local image or their incense censor to the main temple to be reinvested with the spiritual power (*ling*) of the main image. This practice suggests that images are important but fragile loci for the spiritual power and presence of the deity; the concentration of *ling* in the locus of the image enables worshippers to pray to the deity, from whom they expect protection and miracles.[6]

Judged by Their Power

萬
神
一
道

The Chinese attitude toward spirits is a matter of faith frequently confirmed by the demonstrated power of the spirits. As Laurence Thompson has written,

> *The gods are alive because they have manifested themselves through their works.* Their spiritual power, called *ling* in Chinese, is the evidence of their existence. . . . Any claim or attribution of *ling* that gains a certain public currency may result in deification of a person. Rumors having spread and credibility having been established through confirmation that the spirit responds to prayers, a temple will be put up through public subscription. From then on the growth or decline of the cult is a matter of god's efficacy. This means that the death of the gods is also commonplace. When public confidence in the power of a deity has waned, he will be neglected and eventually forgotten.[7]

The continual judging of deities according to their demonstrated power is the distinguishing mark of the Chinese worship of spirits. This accountability is not confined to illiterate worshippers. Valerie Hansen recounts an example of a Sung dynasty magistrate using the principle in his attempts to recruit spiritual support for ending a drought.

> An 1107 inscription from Liyang county, Jiangsu, reports that a district magistrate unsuccessfully prayed for rain at each of the nearby temples during a long drought. Upon consulting a local history, he learned about a temple twenty li to the northeast where the resident deity had always responded to entreaties. He prayed there, and rain followed.[8]

The magistrate consulted a local history, while the illiterate populace depended on word-of-mouth reports on which deities were able to deliver each boon. The principle was the same.

Chinese worshippers expected accountability on the part of a deity, or at least ongoing evidence of active spiritual presence. They understood that deities whose images or temples were in disrepair, or whose offerings were too meager, required more active worship and support in order to produce miracles. However, if the worshippers were doing their part and the deity still did not respond, it was assumed that the deity had lost its powers or was no longer present. For instance, a deity who did not respond to prayers to end a drought might first be

萬
神
一
道

exposed in the noonday sun of the marketplace to get a taste of the drought and then summarily dumped into the river for having lost her or his power to protect the people.[9]

The people relied on the deities to deal with serious life disasters. As Hansen has written,

> Whenever illness befell individuals or epidemics struck entire towns, whenever drought, locusts, or torrential rain hit agricultural communities, and whenever marauding troops or bandits threatened settlements, Chinese people who had no other means of tackling these problems looked to the gods for protection.[10]

A large-scale or serious disaster for which prayers did not bring immediate solace might cause the local community to pull out the stops and consult every specialist or deity they could think of, sometimes simultaneously.

> A drought occurred in Fuchou (Fukien), and a respected member of the gentry led a procession of Buddhist monks, Taoist practitioners, spirit mediums, and three hundred peasants to pray for rain at a well thought to be the residence of the local dragon.[11]

If the purpose of the gods was to protect people from the ailments of life and the afterlife, then major ills might require multiple protection.

The Western observer of these practices is often curious about how seriously the Chinese believed in these deities. Valerie Hansen, in dealing with this issue, cites a number of incidents of authors or storytellers who express a certain skepticism, cynicism, or detachment about the gods, but she notes of one of these skeptics, "Once he himself is in danger, he, like the sailors [about whose practices he was skeptical], begs the gods for help."[12] Having few tools at their disposal to deal with life's challenges, the traditional Chinese relied heavily on their gods.

The Need for Many Gods in the Local Religious Field

For the vast majority of traditional Chinese, the world thronged with ghosts or demons (*kuei*) and spirits or deities (*shen*), who—if properly propitiated—could assist them through the vicissitudes of human life. Even educated persons, who might harbor skepticism about the stories and powers attributed to deities, seldom dismissed the gods entirely. As Hansen comments about two skeptics, "For both, however, the hazards of life—be they in the course of an official's daily routine or on a perilous ocean voyage—were so great that they could not pray to just one god."[13]

萬
神
一
道

The Chinese religious field pulsated with spiritual forces. At one level were the ghosts and spirits, the souls of all who had lived, inhabiting graves, spirit-tablets in ancestral shrines, the fields and glens, the heavens and the hells. Particularly worthy spirits might become deities in the heavenly pantheon. A person's spirit (*shen*) was the imaginative, transcendent aspect of the human mind-and-heart, which—if properly cultivated—could develop considerable intelligence, wisdom, and prowess. Every human being had multiple connections to spirits and ghosts: they were one's ancestors or the ancestors of the community; they were powerful or malevolent deities or demons from human history; they were the spiritual and demonic aspects of one's self. The great Confucian thinkers even liked to depict the terms "spirits" (*shen*) and "ghosts/demons" (*kuei*) as the expansive or contractive aspects of the human mind, or even the expansive and contractive breaths of the cosmos as a whole.[14]

Add to this throng of spiritual beings an ancient belief that the land of China itself was animated by veins of auspicious and malevolent energy which might attract the habitation of positive spirits or malevolent demons. Human use or domestication of the land (particularly for homes or graves) had to be respectful of the spiritual forces of the land. Understanding and tapping the positive benefits of the spiritual forces of the land was the domain of geomancy (*feng-shui*), a protoscience for planning the location and orientation of graves, homes, and other buildings to accord with the forces of the land. Depending on the appropriateness of their gravesites, the honor accorded them by the memorials of their descendants, and the cumulative deeds of their human lives, the spirits of the dead could become benevolent protectors, hungry ghosts, or angry demons who threatened all living beings.

To manage this crowded and complex world of spiritual forces one needed an array of effective rituals. It was not unusual for participants in the Chinese religious field to combine more than one level of "spiritual management" in caring for the welfare of the living, the newly dead, and the ancestors. Given the myriad religious practices and traditions open to the Chinese, and the lack of an obligation to choose among them, the religious location of a person or community in the Chinese religious field was remarkably fluid and functional, shifting with needs and circumstances. One assumed multiple religious locations and roamed the field at will. The multiple locations reflected the multiple roles and responsibilities of a particular person or family. As the place of the family and the individual in Chinese society became more complex, so did the religious and ritual obligations attendant upon them.

萬
神
一
道

The spirit world and human approaches to it were extensions of the human world; religious patterns of behavior sustained and reinforced social patterns of behavior in the culture. In a famous article, anthropologist Arthur Wolf deftly captured the general pattern of worship and offering which encoded the practices of Chinese religious life. According to Wolf, three classes of spirits were worshipped in different places, under different circumstances, with different offerings, and by different officiants. An analysis of the differences among the three classes of spirits suggests a clear cultural code: gods were approached with the deference, courtesies, and offerings appropriate to public officials and rulers; ghosts were treated like bandits, beggars, and bullies, kept at bay through bribes offered out the back gate; ancestors were treated like honored family elders, included in family banquets and celebrations.[15] Thus the vast range of deities and of styles of rituals reflected and maintained the structures of Chinese society.

A Moral Continuum

Chinese popular deities were very often former human beings. These could be moral exemplars who had attained a spiritual appointment after death or they could be locals whose lives had been cut off prematurely. After death, their tombs gave off auras or they would appear in dreams to announce their powers.[16] The careers of these deities depended on their powers in answering prayers and on their moral attainments. Gods, like human beings, remained on the continuum of moral retribution which was basic to Chinese folk beliefs.

Chinese plays and folk tales abound with stories of deities being promoted or demoted because of their deeds.[17] Chinese deities were not viewed as eternally existent beings, but rather as spirits of the dead who have achieved divine status because of their virtue and their development of spiritual powers.[18] In their careers as deities, they continue to be held accountable to a higher power, depicted in fiction as a heavenly bureaucracy under the rule of the Jade Emperor, but also—since the Jade Emperor himself was not a font of perfect wisdom—accountable ultimately to a power higher than all deities: Tao in itself, or the Cosmic Buddha (all reality as Buddhahood), or the will of Heaven. Thus empowering each image is the spiritual efficacy (*ling*) of a deity, a being on a spiritual journey who is seeking, like the faithful who worship him, to embody as fully as possible the Tao in itself.

If the gods were subject to the same moral principles as humans, then tales of the gods also had a moral dimension. The best of the gods modeled for the faithful the virtues of generosity and public-spiritedness; ghosts and demons represented vengeful and selfish forms of behavior.

Transcendence and Immanence

萬
神
一
道

The fortunes of deities, as of human beings, rise and fall. The rapidly changing landscape of deities led thoughtful religious persons to posit a source of spiritual power beyond the multiplicity of the gods.[19] Ordinary people did not care about the theological subtleties of the source beyond; they simply judged the gods by their abilities to answer prayers and perform miracles. Seeking evidence of power, they were content to move from god to god to have their needs addressed. The theologians, however, sought to articulate a continuous source from which emanated the myriad spirits.

The Chinese accepted the reality that it would be impossible for human beings to pray to, relate to, or depict Tao, Buddha, Heaven, the Way, the Truth as they were in themselves, because any such attempt would inappropriately limit and constrain the vast cosmic reality within a specific set of terms and categories. This is most famously stated in chapter 1 of the *Tao te ching*:

> The way that can be spoken of
> Is not the constant way;
> The name that can be named
> Is not the constant name.
> The nameless was the beginning of heaven and earth;
> The named was the mother of the myriad creatures.[20]

Even in this statement, Lao Tzu acknowledges that the named (the embodied) is necessary as a connection with the myriad creatures; yet it is not the thing in itself.

Alongside this notion of the transcendent Tao beyond all human depictions, categories, and names—indeed beyond all attributes of personality—is a conviction that the Tao is both utterly transcendent and ineffable and at the same time is *everywhere*. The latter point is graphically captured by the great "Taoist" writer Chuang Tzu in his famous exchange with Master Tung-kuo:

> Master Tung-kuo asked Chuang Tzu, "This thing called the Way—where does it exist?
> Chuang Tzu said, "There's no place it doesn't exist."
> "Come," said Master Tung-kuo, "you must be more specific!"
> "It is in the ant."
> "As low a thing as that?"
> "It is in the panic grass."
> "But that's lower still!"
> "It is in the tiles and shards."

萬
神
一
道

"How can it be so low?"

"It is in the piss and shit!"

Master Tung-kuo made no reply.[21]

Between the ineffable, transcendent, and unapproachable Tao, and the radical ubiquity of Tao's presence in even what seems most vile and least sacred, is the world of humans and of spirits. The myriad deities are like us humans when compared to the Tao in itself; they are like us in many ways, and thus are approachable with our hopes, fears, praise, and petitions. As in the case of the images discussed in the beginning of the chapter, personified deities were concentrations or loci of spiritual power accessible to worship and petition.

The plethora of spirits and divinities creates a complex religious cosmology, a picture of heaven and hell. If the Chinese religious field were to be negotiated by the faithful, this multiform spiritual world had to be mapped so that ordinary people could find their way. This was done in temple paintings or wood-block prints, in temple or ritual iconography, in religious drama and local stories, and in various teachings and rituals.

One of the most common ways for people to see the representations of the religious cosmology was to visit any significant temple in the community. Such temples displayed not only the major deities whom the temples honored, but also a host of minor deities (local deities, gods of nearby temples, gods of other religions), arranged in a clearly subordinate role, but nonetheless honored and the object of active veneration. These arrangements offered the temple's interpretation of the local religious field and of the religious cosmology.

Religious leaders were aware that popular religious piety and imagination looked for signs of the power and miracles of the gods, and that people cared little for the theological fine points and the sectarian distinctions between deities. Thus even deities with long-standing ties to one religion or a particular school of a religion were also seen as popular deities in a more general sense. Religious leaders encouraged such devotions, because it met the needs of the faithful.

For instance, the epigraph to this chapter cites a monk's justification for encouraging the popular worship of Kuan-yin, even though, theologically speaking, "there is no difference between us and her." He cites the people who "pray on their knees, and tell her of all their illnesses and troubles, and ask for help. Full of sincere emotion, sweat dripping down their faces, they tell her their inner thoughts. The bodhisattva responded to their faith by appearing in a dream." Valerie Hansen comments,

> However undesirable an image of Kuan-yin might be from a doctrinal standpoint, if the monastery is to attract followers, it cannot adhere to traditional doctrine. It must offer the poten-

tial followers a deity in terms familiar to them. . . . Buddhist monks increasingly used the discourse of popular religion, by encouraging the worship of gods like Kuan-yin.[22]

萬
神
一
道

Thus the theological affirmation of transcendence had to be balanced with the popular demand for immanence so that gods would hear prayers and address the ills which beset believers.

The tale of the Taoist *chiao* ritual is a splendid example of this balance between the transcendent and immanent aspects of spiritual presence. It is an outstanding example of how the many gods are united by the Way in a common religious field.

Transcendent Tao and Immanent Deities in the *Chiao* Ritual

Every so many years or to mark a significant turning point, such as the end of an epidemic or the defeat and repulsion of invaders, a Taoist temple and its community sponsored a *chiao* ritual. Readers may recall that Sung emperor Hui-tsung sponsored a seven-day *chiao* ritual at Yü-lung kuan to celebrate the god Hsü Sun's help in repulsing the Jurchen invaders. The *chiao* was the highest Taoist rite, performed to ritually cleanse a community or other site of threatening, corrosive, and debilitating spiritual forces and to renew and reforge its connections to the cosmic source of spiritual wholeness and renewal.

This tale recounts a community *chiao* in Chunan City, northern Taiwan, in 1970.[23] Because of the cumulative grievances of angry ghosts or demons, every community needed a thorough ritual cleansing from time to time; such was the basis of cyclical or regular *chiao*. The survival of a major disaster (such as epidemic or invasion) could leave behind residual negative forces from those whose lives had been prematurely ended by the disaster, and thus also required a ritual cleansing to ensure that the community was thoroughly cleansed of the pestilence.

Since the purpose of the *chiao* was to cleanse and restore the community, the entire community joined in sponsoring it. Every family in the community was invited to participate and to put out its offerings for public display. Participation in this gala ritual event brought the people together around a mutually beneficial common cause; all contributed to its success and all enjoyed the celebration. Deities and special guests from neighboring communities were invited, as were the souls of the dead. Visiting deities were even provided housing in temporary shelters.[24] Souls of the dead were important guests and had to be treated delicately. Their invitation sought to comfort or appease any recently dead who were aggrieved or angry because of ritual neglect; such neglected ghosts could wreak havoc in the community. By inviting and feasting these souls, the ritual integrated them into the posi-

萬
神
一
道

tive spiritual forces who sustain rather than threaten community health and welfare. However, the community did not want such souls or ghosts hanging around indefinitely, so they were given a special ritual send-off toward the end of the *chiao*.[25]

The *chiao* was sponsored by a temple of some distinction, which usually had both major deities (seated in the position of honor on the main altar, facing south) and minor deities (around the sides and the back of the temple). On normal days, the faithful and priests of the temple prayed to these deities for help and succor in meeting the challenges of life. The high ritual of the *chiao*, during which renewal of the cosmos itself was at stake, looked beyond the myriad deities to the Tao in itself as the source of all spiritual power.

In preparation for this ceremony, normally performed by a highly trained Taoist priest,[26] the deities to whom the temple was dedicated and who occupied the seats of honor, were removed to the other end of the temple (facing north) to become observers and worshippers alongside the human participants. As the deities were ritually invited to become observers and worshippers in the *chiao*, the vacated worship space was ritually reconstructed for the special service. In the place of the deities were ritually installed abstract scrolls invoking the Three Pure Ones, three aspects of Tao in itself. The Three Pure Ones were not depicted in embodied form; they pointed beyond the specific and particularized deities of the Chinese pantheon to the cosmic unity of the Tao.[27] In normal everyday worship, the specific embodied deities were the most effective link with specific spiritual benefactions of the Taoist Way, but for returning to the source for cosmic renewal, the ritual turned to the Tao itself, which transcended all particular embodiments.

The *chiao* rituals, performed by the Taoist high priest in the sanctuary of the temple, represented Taoist ritual practice at its most subtle and internalized. The *chiao* consisted almost entirely of an internally visualized set of ritual encounters guided by the disciplined meditation of the priest. These rituals were witnessed by other priests and a select set of temple elders and community leaders. The high priest's external actions provided only minimal markers of the different portions of the rite. There was almost nothing to watch in the temple, and the ritual would make little or no sense unless the witness was already familiar with the structure of the rite and could thus provide the content for different sections from her/his own knowledge and imagination.

The ritual structure of the *chiao* included:
- purification of the temple
- announcement to the Three Pure Ones
- invitations to the Three Pure Ones
- an audience with the Three Pure Ones at which offerings were presented along with petitions

- renewal of contract for cosmic order
- ritual send-off for the Three Pure Ones.

Watching the rite performed in the sanctuary was somewhat akin to watching (without the aid of a prayer book) a pre-Vatican II Latin Mass performed *sotto voce* by a priest facing the altar at the back of the sanctuary! Only worshippers with a solid familiarity with the structure of the Mass would be able to follow in any detail.

If the rite in the sanctuary had been the only ritual aspect of the *chiao*, there would have been little incentive for the community to attend the ceremonies, and interest would have waned. The priestly rite, however, was not the whole picture.

A second set of *chiao* rituals was simultaneously performed in the open-air courtyard of the temple, and viewed by the people of the village. These rituals followed precisely the same structures as the re-strained and internalized rituals in the sanctuary but at a different level:

- purification of the community and of people's homes
- announcements to ghosts and spirits
- invitations to ghosts, spirits, and human guests
- a banquet for human guests as well as ghosts and spirits
- presentation of the community's petition to ghosts and spirits with the signatures of all sponsors of the ritual
- ritual send-off for ghosts and spirits.

The public rites were, by contrast with the meditative, internalized rituals performed in the sanctuary, highly dramatic and popular, crowd-pleasing performances full of color and light, drama and prow-ess, and good feasting. The outer rituals were as accessible and obvi-ous as the inner rituals were mysterious and internalized. Yet they both followed the same structure and enacted the self-same rite.[28] The two levels of the rite functioned both at the level of many spirits and at the level of the transcendent One. Appropriate liturgical forces were invoked in the most powerful and theologically sophisticated manner, and yet the drama of the rite was offered in a form accessible to the entire community.

The cosmic renewal was *effected* by the Tao in a manner invisible to all, but understood by the theologically sophisticated; the ritual was *dramatized or enacted* by the theatrical rites featuring the myriad deities to whom the ordinary believer could relate.

Final Thoughts

The two levels of the *chiao* ritual helped me as a pilgrim in Chinese culture understand more deeply how the rich diversity of the complex religious field held together. The Chinese, I learned again and again, had a genius for letting multiple levels or layers of spirituality function

萬
神
一
道

side by side. The many levels of spiritual practice were all welcomed into one path on Lion's Head Mountain. The followers of Hsü Sun at Yü-lung kung were able to maintain their local religious practices alongside the rituals of the imperially sponsored Taoist rites. In the *chiao* the subtle theological structures of Taoist ritual are externalized into a multi-day popular festival so that the faithful can visualize and celebrate the renewal of the cosmos.

As monk Chiu, in the epigraph to this chapter, defended the cultivation of the popular worship of Kuan-yin at his temple, so all leaders of the Chinese religious field encouraged popular devotion while they developed their theological insights. As Chiu said, "I admire the place she is worshipped and make it imposing in order to augment their faith." He goes on to say that each instant of faith moves the people closer to enlightenment.

My deepening appreciation of the many layers and levels of Chinese worship made me increasingly aware of how awkward I and many Christians have been at acknowledging these many layers and levels in our own lives. How can we affirm our need for more popular, accessible forms of religious symbol and worship, as well as remember that God in Godself transcends all of the symbols and layers? Too often we scoff at "popular culture" religious images as silly or superficial, even as we fail to see the limits of whatever symbols and language we use to envision or approach God.

The interplay of particular deities and the transcendent One demonstrated the tension between the needs of popular devotion and theological speculation. This is a remarkable strategy of the Chinese religious field, and it was sustained by an equally remarkable concept of open-ended or nonabsolute truth, which will be discussed in the next chapter.

CHAPTER 7

Many Embodiments of the Way

> *The Tao that can be spoken is not the eternal Tao*
> *[the Tao in itself].*
> *The name that can be named is not the eternal name.*
>
> —*Lao Tzu*

> *At fifteen, I set my heart on learning. At thirty, I was firmly established. At forty, I had no more doubts. At fifty, I knew the will of Heaven. At sixty, I was ready to listen to it. At seventy, I could follow my heart's desire without transgressing what was right.*
>
> —*Confucius*

As a pilgrim in Chinese culture, I was profoundly impressed by the Chinese genius for bringing stunning religious diversity into a single vision: for weaving the many paths of the Chinese religious field into a single Way (on Lion's Head Mountain, or in any community) or for bringing the myriad deities to whom believers might turn for succor and protection into the all-encompassing Tao or Heaven.

But I was still a stranger, a pilgrim in this foreign land. The more I

"Embodying the Way in Oneself"
These characters (literally in one's body) represent the goal of Chinese religious practice. The Way must be realized in the living practice of each individual.

體
道
於
身

came to know and celebrate the rich multiplicity of the Chinese religious field, the more I began to wonder about issues of truth, or as Westerners tend to construct it, *the* Truth. How did the Chinese respond to the fact that these various deities and religious groups had different teachings? Did not the reality of doctrinal difference destroy the unity of the Chinese religious field? How could the Chinese live with the doctrinal differences without great qualms about lack of consistency? Did they not want to know what, in the end, was Truth? What was the highest or final teaching of the Way?

The Hindus of the Indian subcontinent, particularly those who espoused the school of nonduality (*Vedânta*), argued that the plurality of deities and of realities were illusory projections of ignorance; only the One was real.[1] In China this answer did not suffice. Although the many spirits pointed to the one Tao and the many practices and insights of the pilgrimage were part of one Way, the multiplicity within the Chinese religious field was not taken to be error or illusion. In the Chinese religious field, the many gods, ghosts, and ancestors *were* vivified by Spirit or Tao, and the myriad practices and insights *were* stepping stones of the Way. Multiplicity and unity were *both* real. Reality was both/and, not either/or.

My next challenge as a pilgrim was to understand that the Chinese religious field offered a distinctive notion of the relation of the One and the many, of the relations of the Tao/Way of Heaven/Great Ultimate/Buddha[2] to its concrete manifestations. This notion is key to understanding the affirmation of diverse religious practices in the Chinese religious field.

In this chapter, I explore the significant tension in the Chinese religious field between the One and the many. Philosophically, pedagogically, and in spiritual practices, the players in the Chinese religious field maintained this tension, affirming multiple concretizations of the Tao without either absolutizing the particular or falling into a vicious relativism. One way of understanding this Chinese affirmation of many truths is through the image of *embodiment*.

I begin the chapter with an exploration of the embodiment of the Way through emulating human models, seeking enlightened teachers in books, and following learning strategies of moral practice, recitation of texts, and face-to-face dialogues. I then discuss strategies of teachers which allowed them to point beyond themselves to the Way, and music as a metaphor for the Tao and its concretizations. Finally, I recount strategies for embodying the Way as taught by three great sages of the Warring States period: Confucius, Lao Tzu, and Chuang Tzu. I follow myriad Chinese in looking to the tales of these remarkable teachers to grasp what it would mean to embody the Way.

Embodying the Way

Looking to Human Models

體
道
於
身

One of the most striking aspects of Chinese religious practice is its reliance on human models, living exemplars of the Way. In the Sung (960-1279), Ming (1368-1644), and Ch'ing (1644-1912) dynasties, the imperial governments invoked this ancient tradition to sustain the moral fabric of the society by sponsoring village assemblies which included not only moral lectures but public rewards for local moral exemplars.[3] Carved stone memorial inscriptions honored chaste and virtuous widows, shrines commemorated filial sons and daughters, and popular genres such as illustrated penny-books lionized moral exemplars. The Chinese looked not only to literary and historical exemplars, but also to living teachers who embodied the Tao and its principles in their way of living in the world.

Although theological articulations differed, belief in the living embodiment of enlightenment, sagehood, the Way, spiritual prowess (the terms differ) was pervasive throughout the Chinese religious field. The notion that one might glimpse living sagehood in the person of an enlightened teacher was well grounded in Confucian understandings of human nature and the Way. Following the teachings of Mencius (372?-289? B.C.E.), most later Confucians agreed that human beings were essentially good; they possessed from birth the seeds of virtue and enlightenment. Study and practice cultivated and nurtured those seeds so that the innate positive potential of human nature could be fulfilled in the life of the student. The sage did not represent something wholly other. There was no radical gap between ordinary humanity and the wisdom and virtue of the sage. Achieving sagehood, however, entailed a long process of study, self-cultivation, discipline, and practice.

The forms and schools of Buddhism which flourished in China insisted that enlightenment or Buddhahood was embodied in living human beings: a central teaching of Mahayana Buddhism was "This very body is the Buddha!" In later Buddhism the recorded sayings of enlightened masters had the authority of the Buddhist Truth (dharma) taught by the Buddha in the canonical scriptures.[4] This genre made it explicit that the living masters embodied the same enlightenment as the Buddha. Thus it was crucial to find and interact with an enlightened teacher.

The best way to develop one's spiritual potential was to find a teacher who embodied spiritual values. Such a teacher offered a model for living, as well as guidance and admonition for the student. Lacking a master, one could only turn to books.

Capturing the Teacher in Books

體
道
於
身

Chu Hsi (1130-1200), a great reformer of the Sung dynasty who articulated a renewed Confucian vision, collaborated with another scholar
to produce an anthology of writings of the greatest teachers of his
day in order to attract persons to serious study. Chu Hsi wrote in his
preface,

> Thus if a young man in an isolated village who has the will to
> learn, but no enlightened teacher or good friend to guide him,
> obtains this volume and explores and broods over its material
> in his own mind, he will be able to find the gate to enter. He
> can then read the complete works of the four masters (anthol-
> ogized in this collection), deeply sift their meanings and
> repeatedly recite their words, and absorb them at leisure, so as
> to achieve an extensive learning and return to the simple
> truth.... Someone may shrink from effort and be contented
> with the simple and convenient, thinking that all he needs is
> to be found here, but this is not the purpose of the present
> anthology.[5]

Chu Hsi was careful in this statement. He designed the book as "a
gate" for those without a teacher, but it was only a gate. Genuine study
would involve extensive effort, which was best pursued under the
guidance of an enlightened teacher.

The use of books to capture the presence of a great teacher was the
foundation of the genre of *yü-lu* (recorded sayings). The first *yü-lu*
from within the Buddhist community were collections of *kung-an*
(Jap., *koan*, lit. public case), which formed a distinctive portion of
training in the Lin-chi (Rinzai) sect of Ch'an (Zen) Buddhism.
However, the genre of recorded sayings took hold and spread far
beyond that single Buddhist school into lineages which identified
themselves as Taoist or Confucian in heritage.[6]

The style of these recorded sayings varied according to theological
content and philosophies of practice. Some collections were fashioned
into battles pitting famous teachers against challengers from many
schools or traditions. The battle texts were probably not so much
records of actual exchanges, as they were highly stylized presentations
of the distinctive doctrinal or pedagogical position of the teacher in
question. What these collections had in common was an attempt to
capture the presence of a great teacher. The preface of an anthology of
Chu Hsi's sayings remarks,

> When you read this book, it is like being in attendance when
> the master is at leisure, receiving the tone of his voice. A thou-

sand years could pass, and yet it would be like meeting in the hall, and with the crowd hearing and returning with them to one [mind]. The transmission of this book, how could it be a small contribution?[7]

According to the preface, this collection brings readers into the presence of the master, attending him at leisure, hearing the tone of his voice, experiencing his teachings as though the readers were with the crowd in the hall. Being in the presence of the enlightened teacher provides the atmosphere in which one hears, sees, feels, experiences, and absorbs ideas—embodies them.

Embodying the Way in Oneself

It is one thing, though not a small one, to believe that living enlightened teachers embodied the substance of the Way and could model it for students. It is another to understand how believers were to embody the Way in themselves. Three aspects of the Chinese religious life illumine the process of embodiment.

First, in Confucian lineages study always meant *practice* (application in living) as well as clarification of cognitive understanding. Confucius said,

> A young person's duty is to be filial to parents at home and respectful to elders abroad, to be circumspect and truthful, and, while overflowing with love for all people, to associate oneself with humanity (*jen*). If, when all that is done, young persons have any energy to spare, let them study the polite arts.[8]

Since the polite arts (literature, poetry, philosophy, ethics, music, and calligraphy) were the core of Confucius's curriculum, he insisted in this saying that the active practice of virtue took primacy over formal study.

Nearly two millennia later, neo-Confucian Wang Yang-ming (1472-1529) took this teaching to its logical conclusion by insisting that knowledge and action (practice) were in fact inseparable, two aspects of one effort. He said,

> Suppose we say that so-and-so knows filial piety and so-and-so knows brotherly respect. They must have actually practiced filial piety and brotherly respect before they can be said to know them. It will not do to say that they know filial piety and brotherly respect simply because they show them in words. Or take one's knowledge of pain. Only after one has experienced pain can one know pain. The same is true of cold and hunger.

體
道
於
身

> How can knowledge and action be separated? This is the orig-
> inal substance of knowledge and action, which have not been
> separated by selfish desires. In teaching people, the Sage
> insisted that only this can be called knowledge.[9]

Thus to know the Way was to practice it. Until one could embody the
Way in one's life, one did not know it. To practice was to embody,
internalize, and act out the principles of the Way in one's very being,
to become a living sage.

The second aspect of study which helps to illumine strategies for
embodiment was the *memorization and recitation of texts*. Chu Hsi
noted in the preface to his Confucian anthology (discussed above) that
the isolated student who used this text as a gateway should proceed in
the following manner:

> He can then read the complete works of the four masters,
> deeply sift their meanings and repeatedly recite their words,
> and absorb them at leisure, so as to achieve an extensive learn-
> ing and return to the simple truth.[10]

This statement suggests that recitation was important because it
allowed students to absorb the words. In Chinese, the word *nien*
means memorization, recitation, and study. Chinese students read and
copied texts, annotated them, and wrote essays and commentaries, but
the basic approach to mastering a text was to *nien* it, that is, to memo-
rize and recite it repeatedly.

A recited text was in a very palpable sense absorbed into the voice,
mind, and body of the reciter. In part because of the practice of recitation, Chinese writing was full of allusions and unattributed citations;
the lines, language, and images of texts became internalized as part of
the student's imagination and discourse, his pool of ideas. The text
was no longer bound by its written form, fixed on a page; it became a
sound and image in the mind-and-heart of the student.[11]

Significantly, the word *nien* was also used in various forms of meditation in China which involved invoking the name of a Buddha, a sage,
or a sutra. Pure Land Buddhists practiced *nien-fo*, calling on the name
of Amitabha Buddha; this *nien* or invocation was both a continuous
prayer for the aid of the Buddha and a visualization, a holding of the
Buddha or of an image of the Pure Land in one's mind through repeti-
tion of the name.

Ming dynasty thinker Lin Chao-en, who expounded the unity of
Confucianism, Buddhism, and Taoism, taught the practice of reciting
(*nien*) the phrase "Masters of the Three Teachings." As he wrote, "It
will be as though the reciters were standing in attendance on them
[the masters]; they will not dare to be lax even for a moment."[12]
Recitation absorbed into the self the presence of what was recited; it

held that image (Masters of the Three Teachings, Amitabha Buddha, the Pure Land) in the mind and focused attention on it. In the Chinese religious field, recitation was a simple form of meditation (concentrated attention) which helped students to absorb their objects of study and emulation.

體
道
於
身

A third dimension of study in the Chinese religious field was the dominant image of learning as a one-on-one conversation or *dialogue between an enlightened teacher and a student.* There is ample evidence that other forms of learning were also practiced,[13] but the dominance of the genre of recorded sayings (*yü-lu*) in late traditional China sustained the notion of the learnèd dialogue as a cultural ideal of true learning. By presenting the thought of the masters primarily as one-on-one exchanges, the recorded sayings modeled an approach to learning in which each student's internalization of the Way was tested with and against the teacher.

The three techniques of practice, recitation-and-internalization, and face-to-face dialogue were patterns followed widely in the Chinese religious field with appropriate variations for differences among groups or teachers.

The Chinese did not see the body as an obstacle to spiritual fulfillment; it was rather the medium of its own transformation. The human self as embodied could, through appropriate practice, realize its link with the structures of reality, the powers of the cosmos, and the innate virtues of Heaven. The goal of religious learning and practice was to understand arts for the embodiment of the Way as taught by one's enlightened master and one's lineage.

Pointing beyond Any Single Concretization of Tao

The Chinese were not unaware of the dangers of confusing the immanent, embodied Way with the Tao in itself. They were also well aware that the stress on human models could lead to rigidity and formalism, to thoughtless imitation of others instead of embodying the Way in one's self. Chinese teachers and masters from all of the streams in the religious field, aware of these dangers, used a variety of techniques to point beyond themselves, even as they served as models by means of the distinctive patterns of their traditions.

One way that masters pointed beyond themselves was through their humility, meticulously refusing to ascribe to themselves any title which suggested final enlightenment: sage, Buddha, immortal, perfected one, etc. Masters evaded honors by pointing their students back to ancient masters as well as to the texts, rituals, and spiritual practices which were the core of the curriculum.

A second means by which masters pointed beyond themselves was to avoid making a definitive statement of their teaching. What they

體
道
於
身

offered instead was a series of nuanced statements which spoke to specific circumstances, powerfully adapting the Tao to the particular person with whom they were speaking.

This point can be illustrated by the vast anthology of Chu Hsi's sayings by categories (*Chu-tzu yü-lei*). This collection was immense: thirteen large, Western-style volumes, with sections containing long strings of sayings on a given doctrinal issue. Modern scholars have sought to distill and to summarize the essential teachings of Chu Hsi, since the long strings of sayings impede a general understanding of Chu's thought. Yet the collection was extremely important among traditional students of Chu Hsi precisely because it contained the nuances of his remarks on the same subject in a variety of circumstances to a variety of interlocutors. The sayings were not dated, so they were not studied in order to understand the evolution of Chu Hsi's ideas. They demonstrated rather the *adaptation* of his thought in many contexts, the shades and nuances which made the understanding of his teachings more complex rather than simpler. They showed a teacher who did not simply repeat a set of ideas in a parrot-like manner, but rather adapted them to a range of dialogical contexts.

There was no definitive single statement of Chu Hsi's position in his own writings because *such a summative statement would separate his vision from its embodiment in particular contexts*. His capacity to speak to myriad circumstances demonstrated his masterful understanding of the Way. The question was not simply "What did Chu Hsi say about x?" but rather "what would Chu Hsi say about x in this circumstance?"

The Chinese sought and depicted the Way by means of living exemplars and concrete instances of exchange between teacher and pupil. However, if teachers were incarnate in their expression of the Way, they did not constrain it with all the limitations of a particular embodiment. A given situation, saying, or master embodied the Way, *but not the whole Way*. The Way was concretized only in a particular circumstance or for a particular human personality.

The Multidimensional, Multilayered Way

All human embodiments of the Way were important as models. Yet they were partial in the sense of being neither final nor definitive, but rather limited by particularity and circumstance. The Way, as it unfolded, could and would be embodied in myriad circumstances, but never finally or completely so.

This aspect of Tao was discussed in chapter 6, where the myriad spirits were seen to be concretization of Tao, Spirit, or Heaven, *but with limited functions and influence*. It was also discussed in chapter 2, where the many paths of the Chinese religious field were seen to be part of the Tao, yet each needed to be sloughed off as its limited functions were realized and transcended. The pattern is consistent: *multiple concretizations or embodiments of Tao actualize it in the world, but each of these actualizations is particular and therefore partial.* The Way is open-ended.

Five hundred years before Wan Yong-ming and Lin Chao-en and a century before Chu Hsi, the Chinese poet Su Shih (1037-1101) suggested music as a metaphor for the Tao. This is an intriguing and useful image. The Tao is comprised of a structured set of forces or principles which form the normative grid of reality, like the tones, rhythms, and harmonies of music. Yet the possibilities for expression of music (or the Tao) are infinite; even the greatest musician in the world cannot exhaust them. A great musician may set new standards and inspire many with the potentiality and beauty of music; yet, inevitably, others will both build on and surpass what that musician did as well as honor it by emulating the genius of his or her achievement.

Music is also an apt metaphor because it is only an empty structure *except as performed*, as captured in a particular instance with its distinctive subtleties and interpretations. The structure exists to be performed by others, but the music is manifested or actualized only in performance. Su Shih wrote that the Tao is like music and practicing it is like playing the flute.

> Cut bamboo to make a flute. Hollow it out and blow into it. Even [the great musician] Shih K'uang was unable to fully realize the variations of harmony and descant, the measures of tone and rhythm. Now go back and seek it [i.e., the origin]. There are only five notes and twelve tones [in Chinese music]. At the origin of the five notes and twelve tones there is only whistling. At the origin of the whistling there is only silence. Did not those who made music in antiquity necessarily stand in the midst of silence?[14]

Su Shih's poetic evocation of the nature of the Tao suggests its open-endedness while maintaining its role as the source and structure of all being.

Tales of Embodying the Way: Advice from the Sages

This chapter has discussed a number of ways in which teachers and students sought to embody the Tao. The most venerable models for such embodiment were found in the great teachers of the Warring States period of religious debate: Confucius and the two Taoist philosophers, Lao Tzu and Chuang Tzu. While all three were important models in Chinese religious history, the primary sources of their writings do not offer a narrative of the lives of these great sages. Rather, they record the sayings of Confucius, the poetry of Lao Tzu, and the witty stories told by Chuang Tzu. Confucius's sayings describe him and his disciples in very brief vignettes. Lao Tzu's poetry is sometimes in the voice of the first person ("I"), and sometimes the third. Chuang Tzu's stories make use of a range of colorful characters. All of these sources suggest strategies for embodying the Way. Because of the lack of narrative lives, my tales about these three sages are perhaps best thought of as sketches. They are my impressionistic renderings, drawn from my encounters with these texts and traditions as a pilgrim.

Confucius the Sage

Perhaps the most famous and most honored of all teachers in Chinese history was Confucius. He was revered for his general approach to life and for his wise interactions with his pupils and disciples.

The book which centrally honored Confucius the teacher was the *Lun-yü* (Analects or Sayings of Confucius). The one thread which ran through all of his teachings was declared by one disciple to be "loyalty and reciprocity,"[15] general moral principles which were illustrated in myriad ways throughout the book, but not central to any development or plot. The *Analects* offered brief glimpses of Confucius as a teacher and as a man.

As a teacher, Confucius insisted that learning was primarily about refining character and practicing morality. He expected his students to participate actively in this quest for learning and wisdom. He said,

> I won't teach someone who is not anxious to learn, and will not explain to one who is not trying to make things clear to him-/herself. If I hold up one corner of a square and the person cannot come back to me with the other three, I won't bother to go over the point again.[16]

His students looked to him for instruction and encouragement, and also as a human standard, a model to which to aspire. His disciple Yen Hui said,

> The Master is very good at leading a person along and teaching him or her. He has broadened me with culture, restrained me with ritual (*li*). I just could not stop myself. But after I have exhausted every resource, there still remains something distinct and apart from me. Do what I can to reach his position, I cannot find the way.[17]

The glimpses of Confucius's personality portray him as a gentle and humane person.

In his leisure hours, Confucius was easy in his manner and cheerful in his expression. . . .

Confucius was gentle yet firm, dignified but not harsh, respectful yet well at ease.[18]

體
道
於
身

Confucius took as his mission the returning of the misguided rulers of his day to a path of virtue, but he was not successful in that endeavor. Nonetheless he remained steadfast in his faith in Heaven as the moral source of the Way of the ancestors, which he believed was the basis of a sound society. After failing as a political advisor, he devoted his life to learning and to teaching, never claiming the wisdom or stature of a sage, but coming to represent it not only to his disciples, but also to many generations throughout Chinese history. Confucius claimed no unique or new teaching ("I am a transmitter and not a creator. I believe in and have a passion for the ancients"[19]), but merely to be a lover of learning and of the Way ("Having heard the Way [*Tao*] in the morning, one may die content in the evening"[20]).

The learning to which Confucius devoted his life was not simply the mastery of a body of knowledge, nor a set of intellectual skills, but the refinement of character through the perfection of human wisdom and behavior. The character of a person, Confucius believed, was slowly carved and polished like a jade stone until its inner luminescence shone through.[21] This was a life-long process, even for Confucius, who was regarded as the finest exemplar of his teaching. This is best illustrated in his famous saying on lifelong cultivation, which served as the epigraph to this chapter. No other single comment so aptly captures the Confucian vision of the Tao as the fine art of living authentically.

The Taoist Sages

Lao Tzu and Chuang Tzu, the great ancient authors whose teachings have inspired and shaped the Taoist streams in the Chinese religious field, disagreed with the specific content of Confucian teachings about the sage, but agreed that some extraordinary individuals embodied the Tao. Chuang Tzu wrote,

The sage penetrates bafflement and complication, rounding all into a single body, yet does not know why it is inborn nature. The sage returns to fate and acts accordingly, using Heaven as a teacher, and people follow after, pinning labels [like 'sage'] on him or her.

The sage has never begun to think of Heaven, has never begun to think of human beings, has never begun to think of a begin-

體
道
於
身

ning, has never begun to think of things. The sage moves in company with the age, never halting; wherever he or she moves there is completion and no impediment. Others try to keep up with the sage, but what can they do?[22]

If the sage or teacher modeling him- or herself on Confucius devoted a lifetime to learning and to refining and polishing character, Chuang Tzu's sage devoted him/herself to forgetting and simplifying until the self became invisible or simply united with the world and things. One of the most famous tales illustrating this is Chuang Tzu's story of Woodworker Ch'ing.

> Woodworker Ch'ing carved a piece of wood and made a bell stand, and when it was finished, everyone who saw it marveled, for it seemed to be the work of gods or spirits. When the marquis of Lu saw it, he asked, "What art is it you have?"
>
> Ch'ing replied, "I am only a craftsman—how could I have any art? There is one thing, however. When I am going to make a bell stand, I never let it wear out my energy. I always fast in order to still my mind. When I have fasted for three days, I no longer have any thought of congratulations or rewards, of titles or stipends. When I have fasted for five days, I no longer have any thought of praise or blame, of skill or clumsiness. And when I have fasted for seven days, I am so still that I forget I have four limbs and a form and body. By that time, the ruler and his court no longer exist for me. My skill is concentrated and all outside distractions fade away. After that I go into the mountain forest and examine the Heavenly nature of the trees. If I find one of superlative form, and I can see a bell stand there, I put my hand to the job of carving; if not, I let it go. This way I am simply matching up 'Heaven' with 'Heaven.' That's probably the reason that people wonder if the results were not made by spirits."[23]

Ch'ing, as an artisan, would be an unlikely Confucian sage, for he lacked training in the polite arts; but his Taoist wisdom is based on stilling himself, forgetting, and becoming an agent of matching "Heaven" with "Heaven." Lao Tzu went so far as to depict the sage as an infant, or a fool:

> The multitude are joyous
> As though feasting after the Great Sacrifice
> Or going up to the Spring Carnival.
> I alone am inactive and reveal no signs,
> Like a baby that has not yet learned to smile,

Listless as though with no home to go back to.
The multitude all have more than enough.
I alone seem to be in want.
My mind is that of a fool — how blank!
Vulgar people are clear.
I alone am drowsy.
Vulgar people are alert.
I alone am muddled.
Calm like the sea;
Like a high wind that never ceases.
The multitude all have a purpose.
I alone am foolish and uncouth.
I alone am different from others
And value being fed by the mother.[24]

體
道
於
身

The wisdom, freedom, and behavior of the Taoist sage transcend conventional wisdom; the Taoist sage appears murky and indistinct. If the Confucian enlightened teacher served as a clear glimpse of or window on the Tao, the Taoist sage fogged the window; the Taoist teacher undercut expectations and withdrew from clear view to keep students from seeking a premature handle on what requires extensive unlearning to achieve. The teacher or the sage became invisible so that things could unfold naturally. Lao Tzu wrote,

The best of all rulers is but a shadowy presence to his subjects. . . .
When his task is accomplished and his work done
The people all say, "It happened to us naturally."[25]

The Taoist student learned to still, forget, or strip away all sorts of conventional wisdom, views, and values so that the Tao within could be manifest. He or she had to penetrate surface appearances to uncover a deeply internal reality.

Confucius, Lao Tzu, and Chuang Tzu did not agree on how best to embody the Way, but they did agree that embodying it in oneself was the goal of life. This principle they shared with all members of the Chinese religious field.

Final Thoughts

The notion of truth as embodied, of the Tao as the art of living authentically, provided the opening to allow for the co-existence of many versions of the Way. The Way as embodied is always particular and limited; yet the embodied Way participates in the Way in itself.

體
道
於
身

The Chinese approach to truth entailed humility about the limitations of any single articulation of doctrine and an openness to the fact that truth will never be exhausted as long as human beings live in a world of changing circumstances. As Lao Tzu said in the epigraph to this chapter, "The Tao that can be spoken is not the eternal Tao." Religious persons could disagree strongly and fundamentally on how best to embody the Way in a particular circumstance, but none could claim to articulate a final and definitive statement of the Tao.

The Chinese approach to truth also underscored the life-long art of religious cultivation, so eloquently described in Confucius's epigraph to this chapter. Like the skill of the musician, there is no absolute end-point to the artistry of spiritual practice.

The Chinese approach to truth as embodied or performed was one of the most profound boons I received as a pilgrim in Chinese culture. It stretched my mind and my patterns of religious thinking more than anything else I encountered in the Chinese religious field. The Chinese had devised a remarkable passage between the Scylla of absolutism and the Charybdis of relativism. Too many Western Christians were opting for one or the other, and creating a profound rift between those who held the positions.

The Chinese approach suggests that the choice many Christians see between exclusivism and pluralism is based on a false or avoidable dichotomy, and that the "anonymous Christian" inclusivity of thinkers like Rahner is not the only alternative.

In the Chinese religious field, particular statements and practices could be judged against the circumstances in which they were pronounced—did they further the faithful on the Way? Such was the substance of the liveliest Chinese religious debates. However, even the liveliest debates were tempered by the conviction that the proof was in embodiment: there would be other faithful and other teachers who (like great musicians) would further refine and perfect the Way in their lives.

The Chinese way suggested that we could judge other religions by their fruits (do their teachings and practices give rise to genuine spiritual qualities in persons?), and that we must be humble about the non-finality of our understanding of God vis-à-vis competing forms of Christianity and other religions. It also suggests that certain beliefs or practices might be grounded in, and suited to, specific circumstances; that different teachings need not always be seen in competition with one another.

To my delight my pilgrimage in China was beginning to give rise to insights about my own religious community.

CHAPTER **8**

Hospitality
and the
Chinese
Religious Field

Respectfully on high we invite
The Green Emperor of the East
Wood official who dissolves impurities;
Lord messengers, nine men.
The Red Emperor of the South,
Fire official, dissolver of impurities,
Lord messengers, three men.
The White Emperor of the West,
Metal official, dissolver of impurities,
Lord messengers, seven men.
Black Emperor of the North,
Water official, dissolver of impurities,
Lord messengers, five men.
Yellow Emperor of the Center,
Earth official, dissolver of impurities,
Lord messengers, twelve men.
Ye who bear on high the talisman
That dissolves impurities, Lord messengers;
Ye who carry below the talisman
That dissolves impurities, Lord messengers;
Ye who this year, this month,
This day, this moment bear the talismans
To dissolve impurities, messenger troops,

"Host and Guest"
Host and guest are the key roles within the structures of Chinese hospitality. Each role carries a distinctive set of social and cultural expectations, as well as different connotations of power and status. In ancient times, the terms "host" and "guests" also denoted feudal "lord" and "vassal."

主

客

> *Young men, Jade girls, 120 in all,*
> *Altogether, come down to this sacred* T'an!
> —*An invitation of the spirits of the cosmos*
> *to purify the sacred precincts of the temple*
> *in preparation for the* Chiao *ritual*

In the last three chapters I recounted how I as a pilgrim came to understand the structures for affirming diversity within the Chinese religious field: 1) how the manifold deities, rituals, practices, symbols, teachers, and pedagogical approaches of the Chinese religious field concretized the Way and pointed beyond such specific manifestations to the unity of the Tao; and 2) how the plethora of religious options were held in creative relationship with the notion of a transcendent source and unity, a ground of the sacred. I was deeply moved by the Chinese genius for holding unity and multiplicity in creative and balanced tension.

As I continued my journey, my attention returned to practical issues. How did the Chinese come to know and to negotiate diverse religious options in the religious field? As a pilgrim in China, I was repeatedly warmed by the welcome that I or any other stranger received in a temple or at a ritual. I had first experienced that remarkable sense of welcome during the pilgrimage on Lion's Head Mountain and in the gracious hospitality of its abbot. The sense of welcome was repeated many times at many temples. Instead of enclaves of self-enclosed religious groups, the patterns of religious life created a network of hospitality which sustained mutual knowledge and relationships. How did these patterns work? How did the Chinese come to know about and negotiate the diversity of the religious field?

In this chapter, I explore those patterns of mutual knowledge and relationship, arguing that the social structures of hospitality were key to this pattern of religious interaction. As I recounted in chapter 6, Chinese deities were entertained in the manner of important officials, and ancestral spirits were included in family celebrations and feasts.[1] In the epigraph to this chapter, a Taoist priest invites the emperors of the five quadrants of the cosmos and their attendant spirits to a temple to help celebrate a ritual. The structures of religious practice are shot through with the practices of hospitality, which sustain relationships between religious groups.

I begin the chapter by examining the general structures of Chinese hospitality and illustrating its dynamics at the communal and individual levels. On the communal level, I show how religious hospitality fostered a sense of community, nurtured local leadership, and balanced tensions through cycles of reciprocity. On the individual level, I illustrate the functions and textures of religious pluralism: how persons became acquainted with other traditions and how temples hosted many guests. I conclude with a brief tale of hospitality to many deities and rituals in a temple in Tainan.

The Chinese Structures of Hospitality

主
客

Chinese religious organizations and persons used the structures of hospitality to accommodate diverse religious deities and adherents within their celebrations. They embraced or included their neighbors—divine and human—as guests in their appropriate places and roles. This is, of course, an ancient and virtually universal human strategy for embracing the stranger. The rituals of hospitality and commensality are at the very center of the human mechanisms for establishing relationships across lines of family, community, culture, and nation. And, almost universally, human cultures have accepted the principle that one honors as far as possible the mores of the host: "When in Rome, do as the Romans do." Thus the sensitive guest would not wear street shoes into a traditional Japanese home or refuse hospitality and refreshment from a Bedouin. Moreover, while Euro-American hosts would be offended if their guests were to slurp their soup ostentatiously or belch loudly after the meal, such behaviors would be courteous, if not mandatory, in other cultural settings.

In traditional Chinese society, the rounds of hosting in community festivals exposed everyone to the practices and mores of a range of religious groups and taught them how to handle themselves appropriately in those worlds. They were feted as guests, provided the best that the religious hosts had to offer, and given a chance to reciprocate. The structures of hospitality made the visitors comfortable in their role as outsiders, since they were formally welcomed as guests or outsiders. Thus they could ask questions, listen, observe, investigate, and enjoy; no commitment was asked of them, only their participation as guests.

If the guests were invited as observers and recipients, the hosts took responsibility for defining the terms of the affair. The Chinese term for host is revealing, for it also means "master" or "ruler," the one at the center. Chinese language suggests that the structures of hospitality are hierarchical, with the host above the guest; the host is in control, and the guest is subordinate. In ancient feudal China, the host (*chu*) was the lord, and the guest (*k'o*) the retainer or vassal; as in all feudal systems, while the relation was hierarchical, lord and vassal had mutual obligations. In Chinese society guests looked up to hosts, while hosts bore the responsibility for generosity and providing favors.[2]

What injected a note of equality in the host-guest relationship in the traditional Chinese setting was the principle of reciprocity underlying all Chinese relationships. Any relationship in Chinese society, although hierarchical, entailed *reciprocal* obligations, and none more so than host and guest. The principle of reciprocity promised to reverse the roles, and to place the host in the position of guest, and the guest in the position of host. Host and guest were expected to reciprocate with skill to develop an ongoing connection. Such was the ideal structure of hospitality, and it was one to which the major families, religious functionaries, and officials of a community aspired in the round of festivals. Only through a network of reciprocity could the full potential of community unity and harmony be achieved.

Community Festivals: Reaffirming Cultural Unity

Building on cultural norms of hospitality, the openness to diversity in the Chinese religious field was sustained within a complex web of behavior and practice grounded in the structures of hospitality.

In the long spectrum of Chinese history until the twentieth century, festivals were community-wide events that had as one of their chief aims reaffirming the sense of commonality and unity which transcended tensions, feuds, and conflicts. As each temple celebrated the festivals that were key to its religious calendar, it became the host for a community celebration. The patterns of worship, the deities accorded central honor, and the major patrons of the festival were those of that particular religious institution. If a (Buddhist) Kuan-yin temple hosted one event, a major Kuan Kung (Taoist) temple would host the next. In the cycle of community festivals, each of the major groups had a chance to represent the unity of Chinese religion in its own distinctive way. Each invited the entire community to its celebration, and all members of the community were expected to participate and to contribute to the effort. Since all of the traditional Chinese religious streams accepted this premise of participating in the whole, the system worked well both to sustain community solidarity and to maintain the patterns of openness and reciprocity in the Chinese religious field even in the face of considerable competitiveness.[3]

The emperor or his representative (an official of the imperial bureaucracy) attended significant community religious festivals and visited important shrines or temples in order to incorporate the festival, shrine, or practice into the religious mainstream by virtue of imperial patronage; this presence reminded all religious groups of the emperor's role as the patron of all orthodox religious practice.

The Rounds of Temple Hospitality

As noted above, the rounds of the religious calendar included a variety of festivals, holidays, and birthdays of deities, each of which was the occasion for a community-wide celebration hosted and organized by the most appropriate temple or shrine. The festivals provided the organizing temple with a number of opportunities. The great festival of the temple, with its processions, rituals, and performances, was the key opportunity to present in concrete and dramatic form the Chinese religious field as that group saw it, to depict the religious cosmos with their concerns and their deities in the central roles. To the celebration were invited members of the community, religious neighbors, local worthies, and even other deities and spirits, as depicted in the epigraph to this chapter. However, as is always true in a carefully designed party or banquet, each guest (human or divine) was carefully assigned his or her rightful place in the social and spiritual structure of that particular event.

主
客

This carefully modulated hospitality to other spirits and cults was also reflected in the everyday arrangement of temple or shrine compound. Chinese temples lodged not only images and altars to the primary deities (which were seated in the place of honor in the main hall, facing south), but also images of and altars to a host of other deities. Some of these other deities were assigned places as guardians or attendants to the main deities. These guardian and attendant figures were sometimes assimilated through a process of remythologization, in which what may have been earlier an independent religious group was absorbed into the religious movement or temple as faithful servants of the more powerful deity and its institution.[4] Subordinate deities were enshrined around the sides and back of the temple, or in smaller sub-shrines or buildings. The exact position of each in the pantheon was indicated by its spatial placement, its size and decoration, and the size and degree of ornamentation in its ritual apparatus. The presence of multiple deities established alliances with small religious movements or simply provided broader religious options for those who visited the temple. Thus the temple itself played host to selected deities who were seated in their appropriate places. On the temple's turf, their deity was the host and thus at the pinnacle of the structure of the event.

places for deities

Patronage and Leadership

Each temple or shrine not only represented distinctive practices, deities, priests, and adepts, but also was supported by a group of local patrons, families who had related themselves to the temples as "members of the register."[5] Such families made contributions of land, clothing, food, or money, and also were active on temple committees. The planning for a festival or celebration involved the major temple patrons in many ways, and thus provided them an opportunity to develop their role as community leaders.[6] The introduction of a new temple or cult into a community often served as a vehicle for families new to the region or rising in their fortunes to establish their status by exercising visible patronage. Given the plethora of religious practices and deities, religious patronage was central to the survival of a partic-

主

客

ular group; religious patronage was also important to families in establishing their status in a community.

In addition to providing the temple and its deities with their moment at the center, festival planning also provided an opportunity for the major patrons of the temple or shrine to play the host to their neighbors, temporarily stepping into the center of community attention. Temple festivals, like weddings and funerals, offered families a chance to express their largesse, assert their status, and establish their generosity as pillars of the community. Also, as in the case of weddings and funerals, this display had elements not only of generosity, but also of a curiously Chinese form of "conspicuous consumption," a public display of hospitality and celebration meant to keep up with or surpass "the Joneses" or, in this case, the "Wangs."[7]

haha...

Tensions and Competition

The hospitality and generosity of Chinese community festivals had competitive as well as innocently generous elements. Such was always the case in Chinese society, indeed in any human society. The flip side of ostentatious patronage or generosity is jockeying for position as the most generous patron. In the Chinese religious field, families might jockey for social position by vying to offer the most lavish festival, and temples would jockey for standing in the community by having the most elaborate processions, rituals, and performances. As we shall see in the next section, there was community pressure both to include all facets of the community (including one's rivals) in the festival, and to attend the celebrations of rival temples or groups. In this sort of environment, competition was played out through the subtle social codes of mutual generosity. Since the donations of all parties were made public when offered to the gods, there was plenty of opportunity for conspicuous generosity.

The Chinese ritual structures of enforced generosity and of reciprocity in hospitality were key to containing the tensions and smoothing the ruffled feathers of community discord for many, many centuries. Reciprocity was a key because it meant that other temples and other patrons would have their turn in playing host, being at the center, having a chance to shine or outshine on their own turf and on their own terms.

Universal Participation

One of the factors which vitiated the competitive aspect of community festivals by means of the mores of hospitality and generosity was the deep Chinese instinct to maintain cultural unity against all odds: their strong inclination, reinforced by the watchfulness of the government, to make all community festivals inclusive of the entire community. The temple organizers were enjoined by tradition and the sense of fair play (the rules of the Chinese religious field) to invite to their celebrations the entire community and to participate in turn in the celebrations of their neighbors. As hosts, they provided the feast and entertainment. Guests were asked to make a small contribution as a gesture of affirming the importance of the celebration as a community event, as an act of participation.[8] Contributor's names were written on public placards or sheets which were displayed to the participants in the festival before being "sent to the gods" as a report. As Donald DeGlopper has written of festivals in Lukang, "A family that refused to contribute would offend the god, and, perhaps more to the point, would be mocked and scorned by their neighbors."[9]

主
客

Participation in these affairs embodied community spirit. The refusal of a sub-group to participate on the grounds of having been maltreated or insulted by the organizers was tantamount to withdrawal from the community, a very hostile act. Community festivals were times to mend differences, not to display them.

The introduction into the Chinese religious field of Christianity and Islam, which did not share the nonexclusive assumptions about religion, challenged these time-honored patterns of mutual hospitality. Christians or Muslims who exempted themselves from the festivals on the grounds of religious difference were perceived as also exempting themselves from the community. Moreover, in the late eighteenth and nineteenth centuries, the movement of large and relatively diverse populations into Chinese urban areas undercut traditional patterns of mutual participation and disrupted the traditional rounds and reciprocities of hospitality.[10] Thus as China began slowly to move into the modern world, the tenuous balance of religious diversity was strained both by external intrusions and by population moves.

In traditional China, however, community-wide festivals quite literally broke down boundaries between religious streams and groups, encouraging visitations between temples and devotees. They provided some basic information as well, since the rituals, performances, art, and honorary inscriptions of the festival presented succinctly the special powers, messages, and practices of the deities and groups represented by the shrine or temple. The round of participation featured each temple in turn, while enacting the myth of cultural unity which held together the Chinese religious field.

Courtesy Calls: Hospitality Accorded to Visitors

If the round of festivals within a community created a structure for various competing groups and social forces both to express their social

主

客

positions and to be each other's guests, other patterns of behavior in the Chinese religious field created opportunities for individuals or families to learn about and become familiar with the practices and sites of a broad range of religious groups.

Petitioners or Supplicants

Chinese temples and shrines had relatively few periods of formal worship, but were open for visits by worshippers or passers-by. Some, indeed many, visitors to a shrine or temple came to avail themselves of the spiritual services for which the temple was known. Since many deities, not to mention shrines and temples, had established their niches in the religious field by dint of their specialization in a particular sort of religious boon or ritual, visitors often came because of their need for the particular boon which a temple offered. They might have heard of its reputation through a relative or acquaintance, through conversation or gossip at the market place or a tea house, through reference in a story or play, through a performance or ritual at a community festival. In whatever way they came by the knowledge, their visit sustained the temple or shrine's connection to the specific religious boon sought.[11]

Such visitors were supplicants, callers seeking a specific favor from the deity. Like other Chinese supplicants cultivating the largesse of a patron, they observed the general norms and mores of a courtesy call in traditional Chinese culture, in which the deity is understood as the host, the one with the greater power, the master. First, they came with a gift in hand. The appropriate religious gift was an offering, generally some cooked food or drink appropriate for a deity (*shen*).[12] Second, visitors introduced themselves, paid formal respects, presented their problems or special circumstances, sought assistance, and thanked the deity/host in an appropriate manner. If their problems were particularly delicate or grave, visitors might need a well-placed patron to provide an effective introduction, character reference, and sponsorship. In the religious setting, this generally entailed enlisting the services of a priest or other religious functionary who could appropriately represent one's case to the deity or who would perform the appropriate ritual to invoke the god's help. Important petitions to very highly placed deities might well be presented in writing, as formal petitions were presented to high government officials.[13] Thus in the case of petitionary worship, the god or temple played host for courtesy callers seeking boons or favors which the deity had in his or her power to bestow.

During their visits the temple decorations (wall paintings, statuary, inscriptions, and the like), temple literature, the ritual itself, and any interactions with the priests or religious functionaries offered visitors further information about the temple and its distinctive version of religious mythology and practice.[14] Although on one level the visit was a functional and focused spiritual petition, on another level it was a brief exposure to a particular depiction of the spirit world in the Chinese religious field. Moreover, if the boon was granted (if the ritual was effective or the prayer answered), the supplicant became indebted to the deity and to the temple; he/she was obligated to repay the kindness. This indebtedness established an ongoing relationship which might be more or less demanding. The supplicants may have made a vow to the deity, a promise which they would fulfill if their prayer were answered or the ritual achieved its purpose. Even if this obligation were slight, the successful granting of the boon enlisted the visitors as members of the company of those who maintained the reputation and fame of the temple by affirming the efficacy of its deity and its practices.

主
客

Courtesy in Casual Visits: Making Acquaintances

While the most common visits to a temple or shrine were petitionary, others were more casual. Urban or village temples in China were, because of their location and their ample grounds, frequently the sites of markets, theatricals, or other community events. These events were as much commercial, social, and entertaining as they were religious, and thus we must assume that the motivations of those attending were as mixed as the characters of the events themselves. Yet these events drew visitors into the temple or shrine compound, exposing them to the art, the ambiance, the sights, sounds, and smells of temple life. Fundamentally, however, it reinforced the sense that these temples were part of the community and part of the fabric of life. It established their place not only in the religious field, but in the cultural rhythms of the community.

Some temples and shrines were located outside the walls of the city, "beyond the bounds" (*fang-wai*) in the mountains or other places more remote from the everyday cares of the world. Such outlying temples provided an atmosphere suitable for meditation, study, ritual practice, and monastic routine; thus they were appropriate for the training of monks, nuns, and priests. They were often, if the landscape allowed, located high up in the hills or mountains, literally as well as symbolically above it all; even the effort to get there expressed the aspiration for transcendence and progress in the Way.

The spatial remove of these temples and shrines, however, did not totally isolate them from each other or from contacts with those within the bounds of society. In addition to crowds which might appear for festival days or petitioners seeking the special boons of a temple or its

主

客

religious adepts, casual visitors found their way to the temples or shrines in their remote and beautiful settings. Scholars on outings, travelers, or families enjoying a day in the countryside visited temples renowned for scenic beauty, following roads or paths to temples, also traveled by pilgrims, monks and priests, petitioners, and those who had regular business with the temples. Temples established tea houses or pavilions for the rest and refreshment of travelers. Merchants and local families also established wayside stands.[15] In modern-day Taiwan or China, for example, shops or stands near the base of pilgrimage routes often do a brisk business in refreshments, maps of the temple site, walking sticks, and cold drinks for the road-weary traveler. Such businesses have a long history in China.[16]

The temples and the mountains on which they were often located offered attractions beyond the scenery: historical sites commemorated by stone inscriptions or pavilions, remembrances of famous visitors, statues or religious paintings, ancient buildings or ruins, hermitages or studios of famous contemporary or recent scholars. Thus many temples had a religious, literary, and artistic history, in addition to a number of sites of scenic interest. Temples were foci of a premodern form of tourism, and remain tourist or Sunday outing sites to this day.

Visits to temples were made even more memorable for those with literary interests by the Chinese tradition of presenting commemorative poems on such occasions to friends or to the temple. Poems were sometimes penned directly on the walls of temples or of tea houses, but often the group carried paper and ink with them with the intention of a friendly poetry contest. Chinese poetry anthologies and travel books abound with examples of such poems. While these poems might simply commemorate the scenery, they were often laced with more specific allusions about the temple itself and its practices.

Scholars visiting a temple were accorded generous hospitality. During my visit to Taiwan in 1972, I had occasion to experience the modern version of such a visit at a lovely Ch'an temple, where I was invited to tea with the abbot. Naively expecting to have a chance to ask my specific questions about Buddhist life, I was inexorably drawn into the traditional ritual of conversation, in which the questions one asked and the answers received were structured and stylized to reflect a Buddhist notion of courteous discourse about the basics. Thus I learned that such visits were governed by a formal ritual structure of hospitality. In exchange for the tea and hospitality, visitors would inquire politely about the history, traditions, and teachings of the temple. The abbot or priest would do his best both to entertain and enlighten visitors, making use of a brief opportunity for instruction. Occasionally, the conversation would "strike home" for one of the visitors, who might return or strike up a correspondence with the master.

Such outings were primarily pleasure trips, but they were also a medium for introducing travelers, particularly the educated elite, to the range of traditions and practices in the Chinese religious field. They fostered familiarity and general knowledge, as well as human relationships. Even if visitors were not tempted to seek the Way through the particular form of religion practiced at the temple, they came away with a pleasant and friendly impression. Such encounters oiled the mechanisms of mutual openness in the Chinese religious field.

主
客

Hosting Adepts from Other Traditions

There was another significant category of visitation that was key to the interconnections and development of mutual familiarity in the Chinese religious field. Religious masters, monks, and disciples regularly visited shrines, temples, monasteries, and masters from other religious streams or communities. This pattern of behavior runs deep in Chinese religious history. In the *Analects* and other classical Confucian writings, there are numerous stories of one teacher's students visiting other teachers to question them and test their understanding of the Way. Such students challenged their teacher's rivals, hoping to test and reaffirm the superiority of their own master's practices and teachings.

Many streams of Taoist practice encouraged wandering outside of the bounds (*fang-wai*), removing oneself from the city and society in search of a more natural and free mode of living. These wandering Taoists often came upon teachers of various sorts, and not infrequently set up hermitages in mountains where they were visited by other seekers of the way.

Buddhists, given their cultural roots in India, went so far as to institutionalize the wandering of monks and their visits to other temples. In India, holy "renouncers" wandered completely beyond the bounds of society and community. While Buddhism taught the middle way of monastic community outside the normal bounds of family and society, they institutionalized the wandering of monks during certain seasons both to ensure that life did not become too comfortable and also to encourage the exposure of monks to other teachings and practices. There was an established ritual at temples and monasteries to welcome and assimilate monks and priests from other temples and traditions.[17] Such monks and priests were assimilated into monastic practice and entered into conversations with resident monks and priests about the practices and teachings of the host temple.

The above discussion has perhaps given the misleading impression that a monastery would represent a single and consistent stream of practice. That *might* be true if one were referring to the monastery in a narrow way, that is, to the meditation hall and monks who lived in the

主

客

dormitories surrounding it under the direction of the abbot. However, monasteries were located on mountains (or at least on a substantial tract of lands) and the paths to and from the monastery were dotted with temples and shrines representing various levels and dimensions of Chinese piety as well as hermitages of monks and priests in their solitary practices.

Historically, the mountains which housed active monasteries were even more religiously diverse. Mount Wu-i, where Pai Yü-ch'an had his hermitage, for instance, had a long and rich religious history, and the path up and down was dotted with temples, shrines, studios, and hermitages bearing a diversity of Taoist, Buddhist, and Confucian religious streams as well as a host of folk traditions.[18] Thus practitioners of many religious streams lived and practiced side by side. Visitors to one shrine, temple, or studio passed by and sometimes dropped in on others.[19] Each religious mountain, then, became a version of the diversity and complementarity of the Chinese religious field. Such places offered many opportunities for exchanges between the representatives of more than one religious discipline; diverse practices and pedagogical approaches did not evolve in isolation from each other. Some of these exchanges were depicted in collections of recorded sayings, thus capturing the group's perception of their position vis à vis their religious neighbors in the Chinese religious field.

If community festivals brought together all who lived in a single community or region to celebrate the traditions of a particular religious group, the patterns of visitation to temples or shrines provided ample opportunity to cross religious boundaries and learn from many religious groups. Temples and shrines played host to petitioners, casual visitors, pilgrims, and devotees of other religious streams, and their devotees in turn paid courtesy calls on other temples. These rounds of visitation encouraged mutual familiarity, provided opportunities to take advantage of the specific boons or arts of a religious group, and offered a context for exchanges of traditions, histories, practices, and ideas.

Tales of Hospitality in the Chinese Religious Field

Several of the tales I have told earlier in this book witnessed to the hospitality in the Chinese religious field.

The tale of the *chiao* in chapter 6 is an excellent example of a temple festival fostering unity in the community through hospitality. Not only were all of the families of the community invited to join, but also local and regional deities and the ghosts of the dead. Moreover, in the epigraph to this chapter, the deities of the five directions of the cosmos and their attendants were invited to remake the sacred space in which the ritual renewal of the cosmos was to occur. All facets of the community (living, gods, ghosts, and ancestors) were gathered for a major feast of reconciliation.

主

客

The tale of Pai Yü-ch'an in chapter 2 recounted how an individual could come to know and to be connected with many strands of the Chinese religious field. In his wanderings, Pai studied with a number of teachers, mastered a range of Taoist rituals, and became the chronicler of the Way of the Pure and Perspicacious (Ching-ming Tao). Moreover, at his retreat on Mount Wu-i, he hosted many visitors from a variety of traditions. Pai negotiated the Chinese religious field with skill, taking advantage of his patterns of hospitality.

For an understanding of how hospitality to many deities functioned within a major temple, I now share an adventure from my visit to Tainan in November 1971. A friend and I went to Tainan for five days to study as many shrines and temples as we could fit into a brief visit. As we approached a large Yü-huang miao (Temple to the Jade Emperor), we heard traditional Chinese instruments and chanting—sure signs that a ritual was underway. The music drew us behind the main altar in the central hall to the rear courtyard of the temple, dotted with perhaps a dozen deities less than two feet in height. By contrast the image of the Jade Emperor and his attendants on the main altar were significantly larger than life size, seated on an imposing throne.

In front of one of the tiny deities in the back was a large table piled with offerings (tangerines, Coca-Cola, sweet rice cakes, dumplings) and nearby were a red-head priest[20] and two assistants, plus a couple of musicians, undertaking a ritual before what appeared to be an extended family of twenty or so people.

Since the ritual promised to be lively, my friend and I hovered inquisitively around the corners with our camera and tape recorder, exuding friendly interest in the ritual. After a few minutes, we received the blessing of senior family members to record the rite.

The family had suffered a series of economic and health misfortunes. They had been advised by a priest that these ills were signs that a recently deceased relative was in distress in the afterlife. They gathered at this temple to ask the priest to learn from their deceased relative what was amiss so that they could correct it. They were thus sponsoring a rather elaborate spirit-possession ritual which would bring them a direct message from their dead relative, so that the family (living and dead) could be brought to peace.

The first part of the rite, into which my friend and I had stumbled, made an offering and initial prayers to the black-faced deity Chang Tao-ling (a Taoist leader in the second century, C.E.), who would guide the priest in his journey to the world of the shades. After the family had laid out their offerings, the priest offered prayers of invitation and petition, inviting the deity and his attendants to assist him in his journey to the land of the dead.

主

客

After the deity, who had a subordinate role in Yü-huang's temple, had been put on alert, as it were, the priest and his entourage moved into the main sanctuary and made a full report of the day's happenings to the Jade Emperor, who was, after all, the master of the temple. In Chinese popular mythology, the Jade Emperor is also the ruler of heaven and, as such, dispatches the deities of the pantheon as spirit marshals to undertake various assignments. Thus the ceremony in the main sanctuary politely asked the Jade Emperor to delegate his officer for this journey and sought assistance of various spirit attendants to protect the god and the priests on their quest.

The third and most dramatic part of the ceremony, again in the back courtyard, enacted the priest's crossing over the bridge from the land of the living to the haunts of the dead. The bridge was depicted by a small bench covered with a charm painted on blue cloth. Under the bench burned a series of candles to light the way. After the priest had achieved the appropriate level of trance he dramatically danced or leaped over the bridge to the other side, after which his behavior became quite unworldly. He battled with demons and monsters, performing martial steps as he negotiated his way along the dangerous roads of death. He carried with him a T-shirt which had belonged to the deceased relative as a way of "keeping him on the scent." When he finally met and was possessed by the soul of the dead relative, his body convulsed violently and then he slumped forward, twitching involuntarily. His assistants supported him as he began to speak in the voice of the spirit, a combination of mumbles, pants, and gasps which had to be interpreted by one of the assistants.

The message from the departed one advised the family what they must do to correct the situation to bring comfort both to the departed and to the living. At the end of the ritual, the family were visibly relieved and relaxed, for they now knew what was wrong and had a plan of action.

This tale illustrates the patterns of hospitality in a number of ways. First, the family had arranged and paid for what was an essentially private ritual to deal with a family problem. They had engaged the priest and his assistants for the day to make contact with their dead relative and heal the situation. They knew through their local contacts that these Taoists and this deity had successfully brought messages back from the world of the dead. They had chosen this specific deity and the priests of this temple to solve this religious problem on the basis of their established reputations. The success of their ritual reinforced the perception in the Tainanese religious field that such spirit possessions were indeed a specialty of the god and the temple.

Second, they did not directly approach the Jade Emperor, the main deity of the temple. The temple had installed a number of other deities in subordinate positions to the Jade Emperor, and each—like Chang

Tao-ling—had her or his reputation for a specific religious power. The temple had successfully expanded its sphere of cooperation by inviting the lesser deities to have their place.

主
客

Third, the central portion of the rite announcing the ritual intentions to the Jade Emperor had the dual function of acknowledging the host/master status of the main deity of the temple and of educating the family (and me and my friend) about the worship of the Jade Emperor. Although the ritual was assisted by the deity Chang Tao-ling, the Jade Emperor was invoked as a higher and authorizing spiritual power.

Finally, despite the private nature of the ritual, two strangers and outsiders (American women armed with cameras and tape recorders) were invited to observe and record the rite. This level of openness educated us about the practices and beliefs of the temple, as it might have any observer who happened to wander in. Except for very esoteric rituals, most celebrations in the Chinese religious field were open to the onlooker. There were numerous chances to observe the panoply of religious options.

Final Thoughts

In this chapter we have explored how the structures of hospitality shaped the practices of the Chinese religious field. The skills and obligations of hospitality enabled the Chinese to use religious festivals as a means of sustaining the cultural/community unity which was such an important Chinese ideal. They also established various mechanisms through which individuals would become familiar with a range of religious deities and temples, so that she or he could negotiate the religious field to her or his maximal spiritual advantage.

Throughout my pilgrimage in Chinese culture, I was deeply touched by the hospitality of Chinese religions. I visited scores of temples and was able to observe and enter into any ongoing activities almost instantly. I frequently walked in on rituals "off the street." I kept my ears cocked for the distinctive music of a Chinese funeral, often following it many blocks out of my way to observe another example.[21] I followed announcements in local papers and word-of-mouth information through the networks of the *Kuo-yü chung-hsin* language school about unusual rites and festivals, including a spellbinding fire-walking ceremony in the suburbs of Taipei. No doubt my methods for familiarizing myself with the religious field bore some resemblance to those of Chinese throughout history, although the local academy, the marketplace, or tea houses would have been the traditional venue for exchange of oral information.

Never was I more moved by the power of Chinese religious hospi-

主

客

tality than on my pilgrimage to Lion's Head Mountain, recounted in chapter 2. The mountain was inviting to all who came, and it offered something of interest for virtually anyone. Above all, the hospitality at the monastery atop the mountain welcomed all seekers as honored guests. For many centuries, countless Chinese had learned about religion and advanced their religious journey through pilgrimage. My pilgrimage on Lion's Head Mountain and my stay in the monastery planted in my heart a firm faith in the ability of religious persons to welcome each other across the lines of religion and culture. The welcome of my Buddhist hosts inspired me to return with the tales of a pilgrim, exploring the possibilities for hospitality to the pilgrim in our religious world.

PART 3

Bringing the Tales Home

CHAPTER 9

歸根

Christians and Religious Neighbors

"Wu-k'ung," said the T'ang monk, "tell us when we shall be able to reach our destination."
Pilgrim said, "You can walk from the time of your youth till the time you grow old, and after that, till you become youthful again; and even after going through such a cycle a thousand times, you may still find it difficult to reach the place where you want to go to. But when you perceive, by the resoluteness of your will, the Buddha-nature in all things, and when every one of your thoughts goes back to its very source in your memory, that will be the time you arrive at the Spirit Mountain."

—Wu Ch'eng-en,
Journey to the West

Through many dangers, toils, and snares
I have already come.
'Tis grace that brought me safe this far
And grace will lead me home.

—Traditional Hymn 671,
Episcopal Hymnal

As I have recounted in this book, my pilgrimage in Chinese culture was a journey of discovery and delight, of opening to new learnings, of

---

"Returning to the Roots"
This phrase carries a double meaning: it symbolizes the return to the original unity or source in Chinese practices of meditation, and it also represents the "homecoming" of the pilgrim to share tales of the journey with her own community.

近
鄰

deep personal and spiritual growth. I encountered moments of awe and reverence, of trepidation and anxiety, of confusion, of discovery, of hard-won insight. At times the journey seemed endless; I was a long, long way from home, cut off from the familiar, encountering the strange and the new. Although this remove from my familiar texts, symbols, and ways of thinking was precisely what freed me to experience the world of Chinese culture and religion, I sometimes felt a stab of fear about when I would be able to return and act as the cultural bridge I had set out to become. Like the T'ang monk in the epigraph to this chapter, I wanted to know what further challenges I would have to face, how far it was to my destination.

In chapter 24 of *Journey to the West*, just prior to the epigraph, the pilgrims realize that they have covered not even one-tenth of the 108,000-mile journey to the West. One of the companions asks, "How many years do we have to travel before we get there?" Taking into account the spiritual powers developed by the three companions in their previous lives, Pilgrim (Old Monkey) replies, "If we were talking about you two, my worthy brothers, this journey would take some ten days. If we were talking about me, I could probably make about fifty round trips in a day and there would still be sunlight. But if we are talking about Master, then don't even think about it!"

This passage, about a quarter of the way through the novel, is the first indication that the journey is not to be measured in miles, but in insights. If the T'ang monk persists in believing that the goal of his pilgrimage is to arrive at some external destination, then a thousand lives will not suffice for him to complete the journey. It is when he realizes the Buddha-nature in his own mind that he will arrive: his destination is within himself, not "out there."

So it was with my pilgrimage. I would never exhaust the study of Chinese culture; there would always be more to learn, more to read, more to understand. My insights would continually be chastened and refined, nuanced and corrected. But as a writer and a teacher, as a Christian and a North American, the time came to go home. If I had not achieved anything like the enlightenment which would be the end of the T'ang monk's journey, I had at least attained a level of insight and understanding which would allow me to teach and write, to share my tales with others. Perhaps because my journey was not capped with an enlightenment experience, the process of coming home was an extension of the pilgrimage, for now I had to integrate and translate my fragmentary insights into forms that I could share with my students and my church community.

Part of the adjustment was cultural re-entry. I returned home expecting to feel at home and instead felt strange in my own land. My sojourn in Chinese culture had left a deep imprint of experiences, sensibilities, and perspectives that those at home did not immediately understand or appreciate, since they had not shared my experiences. In their eyes I had "gone native" in some respects; I had changed in unaccountable ways. My extended stay in another cultural world also made me see my home with new eyes, the eyes of an outsider in some ways. I had to adjust to the strangeness of the familiar and reorient myself on my home turf. I was betwixt and between cultures as I went through the re-entry process, and nowhere entirely at home. These discomforts passed with time.

My first major step into the role of cultural bridge came when a student on the very first day of my very first course at Indiana University asked from the back row: "Is this course being taught by a Christian?" For a Religious Studies professor at Indiana University in 1974 this was a delicate question, for our mandate was to teach *about* religion and keep any trace of our own religious affiliations outside of the classroom. Without any time to deliberate, I replied:

> I have just returned from three years in East Asia, and I feel as though I have a foot on each side of the Pacific. It's not exactly a comfortable position, but it's the one I find myself in. What that means in response to your question is that my experience in Asia led me to profound respect for its traditions, although I have the humility not to claim to belong to any of them. I also maintain profound respect for the Christian tradition in which I was raised.

Teaching at Indiana University, I became an interpreter of East Asian cultures and religions. Because in order to teach them well I had to convey the coherence of its world view, its beliefs, and its practices, I developed "skillful means"[1] to convey Chinese religious thought and practice to Indiana students. However, because of the ethos of the state university, until I moved to the GTU I was able to dodge the harder issue of the implications of the pilgrimage for my Christian life and faith. This twelve years of grace gave me time to ponder what I as a Christian have learned from my pilgrimage in China.

My theological[2] voice developed slowly and in dialogue with many friends and colleagues. I spoke in theological environments on why Christians should know something about Asian religions. I led retreats on Chinese spirituality for my church. I sought to articulate to a range of faculty and students how I saw my role in the theological curriculum. I stretched the sensibilities of some fellow Christians by using Chinese examples or texts to shed light on a Christian issue. I learned that my responses to the stories and examples I encountered in China were shaped by my personal experiences and history; by no means do I stand for all Christians. However, I also came to appreciate that sharing my Christian reflections on the Chinese experience invited dia-

近
鄰

logue and conversation; it stimulated others to respond to the Chinese examples on their own terms.

In the spirit of opening a conversation, I assume in this chapter a more overtly theological voice. I do not offer a definitive interpretation of the lessons of Chinese religious inclusivism for our culture, for such a move would be itself profoundly inconsistent with Chinese notions of truth. Rather, I share insights and ideas which have arisen from my pilgrimage, inviting others to respond in terms of their own journeys.

Living with Religious Neighbors

> *"Which of these three, do you think proved neighbor to the man who fell among the robbers?"*
> *He said, "The one who showed mercy on him."*
> *And Jesus said to him, "Go and do likewise."*
> (Luke 10:36-37)

In chapters 1 and 3, I rehearsed the historical and contemporary difficulties which Christians face in developing affirmative stances toward other religions. Because of our history of exclusivism and religious intolerance, and the doctrinal and Biblical warrants which have been used to justify that history, openness toward other faiths has been seen as a difficult if not intractable issue. Its intractability is reinforced by the two major ways in which we have tended to construct the problem.

One major way in which the problem has been understood is to ask whether the beliefs and doctrines of the other religions can be reconciled with those of Christianity. Can one remain faithful to central Christian tenets (i.e., have a genuinely Christian Christology) and also affirm the truth of other faiths? When constructed in this way, the only route to a genuine openness to the truth of all faiths is to interpret Christianity in such a general way that it is no longer recognizably Christian to many. Such was the criticism of John Hick's "metaphorical Christology" in chapter 3.

Another major model of interfaith relations has been drawn from international relations. In this model, representatives of traditions enter into conversations seeking to negotiate some limited common ground while defending their own territories. The saga of the Council on Church Union, while limited to Christianity, is an excellent illustration of how the idealism which inspires such discussions can become mired in a plethora of hard details. It is perhaps not surprising that if historical disagreements have led groups to segment off from one another, it will be no easy task to reverse such divisions through negotiation. The issues which caused the divisions have become the defining marks of each community.

Many thoughtful persons have engaged in interfaith dialogues which fall into neither of these self-defeating models, but the history of such dialogue has been slow to create for the Christian community an acknowledged foundation for relationships with other faiths.[3]

My encounters with Chinese religions opened up for me an entirely different approach to interfaith understanding: the simple, pragmatic issue of living with religious neighbors. I did not focus on Chinese religious polemic or borrowing, although there is a rich literature on both. I did not remain focused on how individual thinkers understood and reconciled the multiple religious strands of their lives, although that was the focus of much of my early research.[4] I sought instead to understand the patterns of behavior, the strategies, the diverse motivations, and the cultural incentives the Chinese had for negotiating religious diversity by means of multiple religious participation. The local, community dynamic of the Chinese religious field impressed upon me that the religious field was comprised of face-to-face human interactions; it was a set of strategies for living with one's religious neighbors.

In our increasingly religiously diverse society, this issue of religious neighbors is by no means abstract; it does not affect only scholars and political and religious leaders. Christianity is beset with internal differences, some of which have created ugly rifts in our society. Moreover, neighbors of other faiths are all around us: in our communities, our schools, our workplaces, and even our families. Living with religious neighbors, negotiating genuine religious diversity, is an issue for all Christians, an immediate and daily issue for many.

Living with religious neighbors, then, is an inescapable issue. One can seek to ignore one's neighbors, but that is in itself a way of living with them, though a distinctly unneighborly way. The pragmatic issue of living with one's neighbors encompasses many layers and levels. It begins on a detached, passive level: staying out of the neighbor's way, seeking to commit no actively offensive acts (live and let live). It includes basic courtesy (do unto others as you would have them do unto you). It extends to proactive, neighborly initiatives: welcoming, greeting, small acts of kindness or thoughtfulness, cooperation, favors, or friendship. Ultimately, for Christians, it would entail "loving your neighbor as yourself."

Christian teaching acknowledges that love of neighbor is not always easy or convenient. The tale of the Good Samaritan eloquently conveys this point. In the parable, the priest and the Levite are so caught up in their own religious obligations and notions of purity that they pass by the wounded man, not wishing to impede their own religious agenda. However, a Samaritan, a distrusted foreigner and non-Jew, goes way out of his way to show kindness to the victim. Jesus' parable forces the

近

鄰

lawyer who had asked "who is my neighbor?" to admit that it was the non-Jew, the foreigner, who in the story fulfilled the deepest obligation of all: to love God and one's neighbor. Despite their religious and cultural differences, despite the history of antipathy between Jews and Samaritans, it was the Samaritan who became the model for loving God and neighbor.

The parable of the Good Samaritan offers an important caution for Christians who contend that only those who profess the Christian Way can follow the teachings of Jesus. In this parable, Jesus goes out of his way to remind us that those who profess the Way may not live it, and those who do not profess it may live it.

I believe that Christians are called to develop their skills for living with religious neighbors by accepting and loving them as neighbors. As we become more skilled in doing so, we will develop with our neighbors a level of daily ecumenism in which mutual knowledge and familiarity help us to grow in mutual sensitivity and respect.

The Religious Field: Seeking Common Ground

"In my Father's house are many rooms."

(John 14:2)

The Chinese notion of religious field, so central to my appreciation of the dynamics of Chinese religious inclusivity, is not a model which is readily transferable to our cultural context. In the first place our notion of "field" has to do with tilled land which is owned, which is some individual's or corporation's private property. While our culture has a well-developed sense of philanthropy and generosity, it is no longer tied to the land; there is in current Western practice no "charitable field."

Second, insofar as the Chinese religious field is a playing field, it does not fit our cultural models of the playing field. Our fields (for football or soccer) are arenas in which two teams fight to defend their goals; they are battlegrounds. Throughout Western history, the image of battleground has been all too apt as an image of the exclusivist religious field. The notion of field, alas, does not provide an image of common ground for our culture.

Our primary term for common ground is "community" (its very root suggests commonality, or unity), and an important image is the public square, the center of the community in which public events occur. The public square is, in the tradition of the town meeting, also the ground on which different viewpoints are expressed, where they encounter one another. Community is still an important ideal, but it is increasingly a nostalgic, utopian ideal.

The growth of urban centers has strained traditional ideals of community. The modern city is simply too large for town meetings or one central place of assembly. Neighborhood associations and a host of interest groups have replaced "community" as the gathering point of civic concern and discussion. This patchwork of groups creates a chorus of competing interests which are hard to reconcile in the traditional patterns of building community consensus. Cities are comprised of many competing communities.

The globalization of cities and towns throughout America has also strained the traditional sense of community and common ground. The global diversity brings much richness to a community in terms of cultural traditions, art forms, cuisines, and festivals, but the downside is that the cultural common ground becomes less clear. The traditional religious and cultural classics which served as the common heritage of "Americans" must now be supplemented by the many cultural traditions represented by all of our citizens. Globalization has its consequences.

Still, the community is a primary locus for finding common ground for living with religious neighbors. Many communities celebrate the festivals of diverse cultures and ethnic groups, holding a round of civic events not unlike the traditional rounds of temple festivals in China. Civic leaders are expected to "make the rounds" in order to symbolize and affirm the inclusion of diverse groups in the larger community. In many areas, it is becoming a custom for folks to visit each other's cultural festivals.

In some communities, neighbors join across the lines of faith in interfaith councils to work collaboratively on issues of concern to the community. In Sacramento, California, for instance, an interfaith network of congregations operating a program for youth at risk includes not only churches and synagogues, but also mosques.[5] In other communities, people join hands across lines of faith to fight against the evils of hatred and intolerance. A Presbyterian member of an interfaith council in Dallas reported that her reason for becoming involved in such work was that "Skinheads are vandalizing synagogues in Dallas, and we need to band together to stop these acts of violence."[6] Such alliances against intolerance echo alliances of white and African-American churches to rebuild burned churches and work to prevent further destruction.

In Chicago, a Jewish congregation lost its synagogue and found itself without a meeting place. The leadership made an agreement with a local church to share the church's worship space. The cross is installed for Christian worship, and replaced by the ark of the covenant for Jewish worship. The two congregations worship jointly once a year, after which they meet to discuss maintenance of their shared space. By sharing the space, both Christians and Jews have grown in respect for each other's traditions of worship.

These examples each grew out of specific relationships and events

近

鄰

in a local community and were enabled by the relationships developed between persons of different faiths. The parties involved were creative in discerning the openings for developing common ground. They are small but path-breaking examples, concrete steps in developing a network of interfaith relationships in these communities.

The work of these persons is all the more impressive because we lack cultural images or metaphors to envision the common ground on which we might meet persons of other faiths. The lack of such images or models impoverishes our imaginations and makes it harder to recognize openings for meeting points.

One possible image, though not without its difficulties, is the image of God's house with many rooms, in John 14:2. The potential of this image as a Christian model for negotiating religious diversity was brought home to me (if you will forgive the pun) in a book by Linda Moody. Moody invoked the image of a house from the writing of a secular feminist theorist, Rosemarie Tong. Tong developed her image as an attempt to transcend the bitter divisions within the feminist camp. She wrote,

> It is a major challenge to contemporary feminism to reconcile the pressures for diversity and difference with those for integration and commonality. We need a home in which everyone has a room of her own, but one in which the walls are thin enough to permit a conversation, a community of friends in virtue, and partners in action.[7]

Tong's image builds on Virginia Woolf's famous notion that some private space, a room of her own, is a necessity for the development of woman's consciousness and voice.

It is a fitting image for religious communities as well. For the vast majority of religious folk, the distinctive space of their community provides a much-needed venue of worship, prayer, reflection, and conversation which develops their religious identity and sense of a place in the world. While we seek common ground on which to meet and to celebrate one another, we also need to know who we are and to affirm our communities of choice.

The image of the house can, I believe, be enriched by linking it to the biblical image of the "Father's house with many rooms." However, this would entail an expanded reading of this biblical passage. All too often our reading of John 14:2 is solely individualistic, seeing the Father's house as full of rooms for individuals, and the saying as assurance that we, in effect, won't have missed the housing deadline—there will be a room available for us personally. In the gospel context, Jesus is assuring his disciples that, although he is going away, he will come again for them, and there will be a place for them.

The question, however, is: How wide is God's love? How capacious is God's house? Is it possible that the many rooms in God's house will also have places for those who have found paths to God different from our own? They may be in another wing of the house, but do those who have sought God in many paths ultimately end up under God's roof, in the vastness of God's embrace? We cannot know for certain, but as a Christian, what I have glimpsed of the steadfastness and vastness of God's love assures me that it is always beyond my comprehension, far vaster than my heart or my imagination can reach.

Assuming that God's house has many rooms, there will be room for my particular Episcopalian sense and sensibility, but also rooms for many others. And we as Christians have sound warrant to believe that the reach of God's love will be very great indeed. We are all likely to meet, in God's capacious house, folks we did not expect to see there.

Moody's development of the image of the house of many rooms moves beyond the size of the house to note that the image of a house suggests common spaces: spaces which run up against white middle-class need for privacy. Such folks are a bit cautious about mixing it up. Moody warns,

> It is not necessary for us to have our room completely decorated and pictures hung on the wall before venturing out [into the common spaces]; in fact, it is critical that we move back and forth from our room to common living spaces even as we deepen our own wellspring.[8]

U.S. white middle-class assumptions of privacy in the home have been developed to an unusual point in the second half of this century. In most cultures and classes, indeed in most times in U.S. history, homes were multigenerational and included large groups of family and even nonfamily members. Privacy was minimal; spaces were shared, doors remained open. Moody suggests in a very thought-provoking way that the development of spacious nuclear family homes with a wealth of private spaces has compromised the development of our skills for sharing and opening ourselves to others. We have become intensely private people, and the development of computer technologies may be exacerbating this trend despite their vaunted interconnectedness. God's love not only loves us as we are and invites us to be our authentic selves (and thus provides us a room of our own) but also invites us to ever broader love in the common rooms of this divine complex.

Consider the common spaces of a house: they serve multiple purposes. In the kitchen and dining room, we prepare food either for our families or to invite others to eat with us. The dining room of God's capacious house is extremely important, since commensality, the invitation to share food, is the most ancient and venerated form of hospitality, of entering into relationship with the stranger. In living rooms or parlors, we entertain, converse, or hold meetings. In sewing rooms, computer rooms, or game rooms we come together for common purpose or activities. We meet informally daily in the hall, the kitchen, and the backyard. In attics and basement are items stored from the past, not often used or perhaps forgotten, that nonetheless may be recovered for our own group or lent to another. The common spaces of the house are meeting grounds, places of interaction, or mutual hosting. They can provide chance encounters (for those who happen to be in or pass through the same space at the same time) or intentional meetings or celebrations.

The image of a house with many rooms has some promise as a Western, Christian, biblically rooted model for understanding and negotiating religious diversity in our context. It offers some common ground, but also the assurance of private spaces in which to preserve the particular identities of our various traditions. It does not challenge us to become one or transcend our particularities, only to meet one another in God's love.

The image of the house, however, makes clear that our own rooms are connected to the common spaces under one roof (in the Biblical sense, the roof is God's love); it challenges our instincts to see *only* the private and particular and to refuse to envision or enter the common ground. This model may have some potential to open up our Western Christian imaginations to see new possibilities for living with religious neighbors.

Embodiment

> "And the Word became flesh and dwelt among us, full of grace and truth."
>
> *(John 1:14)*

The Chinese notion of truth as embodied, of the inseparability of knowledge and action, of the Way as not only the highest truth but also a way of life or an art of living, struck a deep, resonant chord in me as a Christian and as a woman.

Although much of church teaching has focused on doctrines or statements about God and creation, the central content of that teaching has to do with Christology and incarnation. The fundamental truth and paradox of Christian teaching is that "The Word became flesh and dwelt among us," was crucified, died, and buried, and rose again from the dead, in accordance with the scriptures. It begins with and grows out of the incarnation, the embodiment of the Word of God in human form.

The doctrine of Word made flesh, God in human form, puts the embodiment of truth, its living out in an actual human life, at the very center of Christianity. There is, to be sure, a fundamental divide between Christianity and Chinese (and Indian) traditions over the Christian claim of the uniqueness of the incarnation. That is, and will long remain, a stumbling block for those seeking to reconcile Christian beliefs with those of other religions. However, the affirmation of the incarnation also opens a broad avenue to appreciating the Chinese approach to truth.

Embodiment of truth goes beyond the incarnation itself, although the incarnation creates a theological foundation for such embodiment. Christians, like the Chinese, look to human models for inspiration about how to live out their faith. They look not only to Jesus, but also to other models: the disciples, famous teachers and theologians, pastors, saints of the church, and other religious figures—Mother Theresa, Martin Luther King.

Moreover, despite our Western Christian proclivities to focus excessively on doctrinal ways of understanding God as opposed to contemplative ways of apprehending the mystery,[9] the history of Christian spirituality provides many techniques and images for internalizing or embodying the sacred. A striking example of an embodied spirituality comes from Hadewijch, of thirteenth-century Flanders, who wrote "The Allegory of Love's Growth." This poem portrays the growth of love in the Christian soul as gestation within the womb. The first month is faithful fear; the second, joyful suffering; the third "raises the number/As the soul thus can carry all,/And it knows that it carries Love"; the fourth is the state of sweetness; the fifth month "brings to effect the most sweet burden that the soul has received"; the sixth month is confidence; the seventh, justice; the eighth the wisdom of Love.

> The ninth month is as if wisdom engulfs
> All that is love in love.
> Then love's moment of power comes
> And continually assaults wisdom.
> As man with all that man is
> Contents Love and is conformed to Love,
> So in the ninth month is born
> The Child that lowliness has chosen.[10]

Gestation is perhaps the most explicit of all images of embodiment, for it suggests that Love grows from the very body and being of the worshipper.

Embodied spiritualities are not always as dramatic as Hadewijch's gestation imagery, and—in the view of feminists—they place the locus

近

鄰

of Christian faith and life squarely in everyday, ordinary lives. Linda Moody has studied the feminist theologies of white, African-American, Caribbean, and Hispanic and Latino women, finding many important and ineradicable differences among these authors. Among the few commonalities was that they all profess an embodied spirituality. She comments:

> In part, this effort stems from a rejection of the abstract theologizing of the past that excluded women's lives. Theological reflection is built upon the concrete, everyday experience of women in each of these theologies. God, too, is seen as embodied, with real concern for the material, physical welfare of women and their families.[11]

The feminist theologians' assertion that the locus of spirituality is in everyday life is consistent with what we have seen in the Chinese religious field, where the particular deities function to assist human beings in dealing with daily and this-worldly troubles. Spirituality for the Chinese, as well as for feminists, begins in the concrete concerns of the everyday, and builds from there to more transcendent dimensions and levels. The Way is rooted and grounded in the body and in the real lives of human beings; it includes the experiences of family and household, of daily life and illness, the struggles and joys of everyday living as its root or base.

One of the contributions of feminist theology has been to recover for Christians the importance of embodiment, the practice or living out of the Christian life. This resonates well with the contemporary (and often unchurched) interest in spirituality: spiritual practices, values, and beliefs. While the popular forms of spirituality are sometimes—in the eyes of those steeped in a particular tradition—fragmentary, rootless, and superficial, the interest in spirituality becomes a potential meeting point between the churched and the unchurched, a common ground on which to open conversation. This is important because living with religious neighbors successfully also means reaching out to the unchurched and the nonobservant, who in some areas are becoming the religious majority.

One of the great potentials of the notion of embodiment for living with religious neighbors is that embodiment is done individual by individual (although often supported, informed, and influenced by participation in a religious community). Because each of us must practice religion for him/herself, we can each speak out of our own experience of practice. We can meet other faithful persons, either from our own tradition or from another, and learn from one another.

In a fascinating development of the late twentieth century, much of the encounter with other traditions through reading, retreats, and workshops is precisely in the area of spiritual practice. There seems to be a strong impulse to find ways to bring faith alive, to revitalize prayer or contemplation, to learn from and about the practices of other religious traditions. Perhaps this is simply another form of self-help, but the pattern does provide an opening or meeting ground for many to become acquainted with other faiths.

Another level of embodiment from which we can all learn are specific examples of interfaith partnerships: marriages, projects, or ministries. Our culture is replete with specific experiments such as these, and we would benefit from attending to them and learning from their experiences, good and bad, about the promise and challenges of living with religious neighbors.

Hospitality

> *"I was a stranger, and you welcomed me."*
>
> *(Matthew 25:35)*

As I recounted in chapter 8, the structures of hospitality were key to the dynamics of the Chinese religious field. Members of various temples and shrines in a given community played host and guest to each other in a round of religious festivals and celebrations. Visitors were welcomed at temples and pilgrimage sites, entertained and instructed. It was customary to pay courtesy calls to temples and shrines, not only because of their historical and cultural interest, but to learn about and honor their traditions and their contributions to the religious field.

The metaphor of hospitality to one's religious neighbors is very promising, for hospitality is a venerable tradition in our culture and religious history. The structures of hospitality define civilized behavior and govern one's relation to strangers. While in the informal ethos of contemporary American life, we often play fast and loose with traditional rituals and codes of hospitality, nonetheless hospitality remains an important means of establishing, defining, and sustaining relationships.

Thomas Ogletree has argued that the Christian notion of hospitality to the stranger is a fundamental metaphor for the Christian moral life.

> To offer hospitality to the stranger is to welcome something new, unfamiliar, and unknown into our life-world. On the one hand, hospitality requires a recognition of the stranger's vulnerability in an alien social world. Strangers need shelter and sustenance in their travels, especially when they are moving through a hostile environment. On the other hand hospitality designates occasions of potential discovery which can open up

our narrow provincial worlds. Strangers have stories to tell which we have never heard before, stories which can redirect our seeing and stimulate our imaginations. The stories invite us to view the world from a novel perspective.[12]

Ogletree's analysis goes far beyond simply being neighborly, acknowledging the existence or propinquity of the neighbor through an act of hospitality. It includes sensitivity to the power dynamic of the encounter: if the other is a stranger in the sense of being in an alien social world (i.e, represents a minority culture or tradition not well understood), then he or she is vulnerable and needs our support and protection. He also notes that the stranger has gifts to contribute to our world, "stories to tell which we have never heard before." The stranger will contribute to, enrich, and expand our life-world in fundamental ways. Thus this hospitality opens us and our world to transformation and enrichment.

Ogletree notes that the stranger represents otherness in all of its manifestations:

> wonder and awe in the presence of the holy, receptivity to unconscious impulses arising from our being as bodied selves, openness to the unfamiliar and unexpected even in the midst of our most intimate relationships, regard for characteristic differences in the experiences of males and females, recognition of the role social location plays in molding perceptions and value orientations, efforts to transcend barriers generated by racial oppression.[13]

Ogletree here suggests that hospitality to the stranger and attentiveness to the other in many forms can accomplish the sorts of goals for which I undertook my long pilgrimage in Chinese culture. We all, he argues, have manifold opportunities to encounter the other, to expand our horizons, to develop our sensibilities to the richness of being in relation to our specific location.

He also notes that in order to realize the moral fruits of hospitality we cannot only play the generous host, putting ourselves thereby in a position of privilege and power.

> My readiness to welcome the other into my world must be balanced by my readiness to enter the world of the other. My delight in the stories of the other as enrichment for my orientation to meaning must be matched by my willingness to allow my own stories to be incorporated into the values and thought modes of the other.[14]

Ogletree's theological understanding of hospitality to the stranger provides a wonderful foundation for Christian hospitality toward the religious neighbor.

近
鄰

Hospitality implies face-to-face relations; it cannot be accomplished simply by talking or reading about neighbors. One must meet them. Through meeting, a relationship is established. If all goes well, trust may be built and may even flower into friendship.

Hospitality need not imply any attempt to convert or co-opt the other. Too often in Christian churches we have seen our welcome to the visitor simply as a strategy for recruitment. Interfaith hospitality needs to be structured so as to allow the guest to be simply a guest, true to his/her values, identity, and commitments.

In my local parish, we are on the verge of establishing interfaith biblical study groups with a local Jewish congregation. We have agreed that what we seek is small groups meeting over food (using commensality as a hospitality structure, with due regard for the dietary observances of our Jewish colleagues), and in groups of equal numbers of Christians and Jews. The numerical equity is intended to keep either side from feeling overwhelmed or tokenized. We will discuss texts from the Hebrew Bible with an eye to understanding our very different readings. We hope that the Christians will become more aware of the Jewish roots of these texts, and that Jews will experience the genuine openness and regard of Christians for the richness of their heritage.

Issues of Truth

> "A sound tree cannot bear evil fruit, nor can a bad tree bear good fruit. Every tree that does not bear good fruit is cut down and thrown into the fire. Thus you will know them by their fruits."
>
> (Matthew 7:18-20)

Jesus' metaphor for helping his followers to recognize false prophets is a useful biblical teaching for considering the issues of truth in interfaith relations. Living with and even loving one's religious neighbors does not mean that one condones that which is against one's deepest convictions and values. But it does require more than looking for total agreement on all points of belief and interpretation. The Chinese would agree with Jesus' metaphor: you will know them by their fruits.

The beliefs and practices of others might be very different from one's own, but what sort of persons do they produce? Can we discern genuine spiritual qualities, authentic moral values, true holiness in the

近
鄰

followers of other traditions? It is impossible to articulate a clear principle of what each of these would look like, but—although this is not a
simple matter—we are capable of recognizing the holy when we
encounter it, even in a new form. As Diana Eck has written,

> Each of us brings religious or ethical criteria to our under-
> standing of the new worlds we encounter. When I "recognize"
> God's presence in a Hindu temple or in the life of a Hindu, it
> is because, through this complex of God, Christ, and Spirit, I
> have a sense of what God's presence is like. Recognition
> means that we have seen it somewhere before. I would even
> say that it is Christ who enables Christians—in fact, chal-
> lenges us—to recognize God especially where we don't expect
> to do so and where it is not easy to do so.[15]

Eck's point is eloquent. If we have developed our Christian faith in
God, that faith will help us to recognize God and God-like teachings in
other venues and forms. It is not a simple test, but one rooted in our
faith and spirituality.

The other important aspect of the Chinese understanding of truth is
its affirmation of humility, of the incompleteness of *any* statement or
articulation of the truth. Theologically, this statement affirms the freedom of God to continue revealing new understandings to us, and the
freedom—indeed the mandate—of Christians to continually reappro-
priate the Christian gospel in the light of new contexts and situations.
The gospel is not a fixed, dead letter, but the Word of God. If we
believe that God loves the world and that the Holy Spirit continues to
infuse the church with vitality, then new understandings of Christian
faith and life will continue to unfold, and our present understanding is
not the final word.

Such appropriate humility leaves open the door to learn from other
faiths insofar as God is present in and through them.

Conclusion

In this final chapter I have cited a number of examples that suggest
that Christians in our culture are beginning to develop creative strategies for living more affirmatively with their religious neighbors. I celebrate these initiatives and pray that we will build on them.

The three stories I cited in the opening of chapter 1 also illustrate
the sorts of strategies which I have lifted up in this chapter.

The Catholic and Buddhist friendship in a Bay Area suburb illustrates two of my points. It started with a similarity of practice: process-

ing with saints/Buddhas on a feast day. Despite considerable theological differences, the similar form of veneration was the opening which allowed Vietnamese Buddhists and Portuguese Catholics to recognize some common ground. Second, the Catholics recognized a gesture of friendship and extended the hand of hospitality to their Buddhist neighbors, thereby creating an ongoing pattern of interaction.

近
鄰

The Tlingit and Orthodox accommodation in funerals, bridging the long-house ceremony to a church funeral by a solemn procession, is important because it is a historical example of neighborly accommodation across religious lines. This is an issue of contextualization, of Christians being willing to make space for the traditions of peoples adapting to Christianity. For many Native Americans and for Christians from cultural backgrounds where religious and cultural identity and practices have been densely interwoven, the openness of Christians to such observances is a vital issue. How open are we as Christians to the rich global identities within our churches? Do we ask folk to shed their roots in order to belong to the church? In this case, the issue of hospitality is not in relation to other faiths and communities, but the willingness of our own churches to welcome the cultural and global richness of its members.

The story of an evangelical church celebrating the moon festival with Chinese international students illustrates an unusually generous hospitality. This church did not simply invite the Chinese students into their space on the church's own terms, but also sought a way to become guests as well as hosts by celebrating a tradition of the Chinese students. The church presumably became comfortable about celebrating the moon festival by seeing it as merely a festival (i.e., not a pagan religious belief). In China the moon festival is a secular festival, but it is also rooted in the religious and cultural values of the Chinese. This raises a fascinating point. The line between secular and sacred is drawn very differently in other cultures. The border around religious issues in contemporary U.S. society is, in the perspective of global world history, a very narrow line, designating only formally professed beliefs, membership, and participation in a specific religious institution. Many cultural observances, such as Thanksgiving, are viewed as secular, although they are profoundly shaped by religious beliefs and traditions.

On the one hand, we need to recognize that what may look to us like secular matters (such as whether a Muslim woman or a Christian Scientist will accept certain medical treatments) may be not only influenced but also mandated by religion. On the other hand, the narrow line we draw around "the religious" opens the door for various forms of interaction with religious neighbors which are not seen as in conflict with our faith commitments.

近
鄰

Living with religious neighbors requires that we honor the religious sensibilities of our neighbors and of ourselves. We will not be able to honor them until and unless: 1) we are each well rooted in our own faith; 2) we come to know more about one another; and 3) we begin to talk face-to-face. May we all grow in the art of being good religious neighbors.

Notes

Prologue

1. I left the Deanship in June 1996, but stayed on to teach and write at the GTU.

2. In the early years of establishing religious studies departments at state universities, the general principle applied by the courts was that departments could teach *about* religion, but they could not *teach religion*. This distinction is still used by some in religious studies.

3. See my "Religious Studies and the Exposure to Multiple Worlds," in *Beyond the Classics? Essays in Religious Studies and Liberal Education*, ed. Frank E. Reynolds and Sheryl L. Burkhalter (Atlanta: Scholars Press, 1990), pp. 179-202.

4. It is not uncommon in theological studies for schools to prefer having "other religions" represented directly by spokespersons for their faith; only then, it is argued, do we treat these religions as equals. While there is merit in this approach, there is also an important difficulty: given the linguistic, symbolic, and cultural gaps between religious traditions, on whose shoulders is the weight of translation? Do we require that Buddhists and Hindus know not only their own language and context, but also our own? Can Christian scholars of other religions who have learned the languages, lived in the cultures, and come to know well representatives of the traditions, be translators from our side? The role of persons like me is not to replace direct voices from other traditions, but to help North American Christians to do our part in building the bridge, in reaching out to other traditions by setting foot, so to speak, on their territory.

5. This phrase evokes the self-understanding of Elsa Tamez, a United Methodist Mexican of mixed heritage, who understands her task as helping those who are not Indian or Black to receive the spiritual practices of others with equality and joy. Elsa Tamez, "Quetzalcoatl Challenges the Christian Bible," paper presented at the annual meeting of the American Academy of Religion, November 1992, San Francisco. Cited in Linda Moody, *Women Encounter God: Theology across the Boundaries of Difference* (Maryknoll, NY: Orbis Books, 1996), p. 123.

6. I acknowledge that every storyteller, whether a Chinese master, a Chinese historian, or myself, selects and reshapes the material through his or her particular lens. It is not possible to convey fully and objectively another context. Although the contexts of the story are filtered both by Chinese tradition and by my retelling, they nonetheless provide some texture, some grounding, for the religious practices or ideas portrayed.

7. The phrase was used by Vivian-Lee Nyitray to characterize the biographies of the *Shih chi*, an early Chinese history. See her *Mirrors of Virtue: Lives of Four Lords in Ssu-ma Ch'ien's Shih Chi* (Stanford: Stanford University Press, forthcoming), MS. p. 11.

8. Thus, like Francis Clooney, I step back from any claim of an encompassing, comprehensive narrative, much less an interpretation which would embrace the realities or truth of both Chinese religions and Christianity. I aspire only to small insights and fruitful suggestions. Francis X. Clooney, S.J., *Seeing through Texts: Doing Theology among Srivaisnavas of South India* (Albany: State University of New York Press, 1996), pp. 299-304. Clooney's work and his distinctive methodology will be discussed in chapter 3.

9. Newhall fellowships are a GTU program which invites collaboration between faculty and doctoral students in the fields of research or teaching.

1. Religious Diversity and the Pilgrimage to China

1. As in Will Herberg's classic, *Protestant, Catholic, Jew: An Essay in American Religious Sociology* (Garden City, NY: Doubleday, 1955). This neat picture left out Native American traditions and a number of small religious minorities, but it represented public perception in the 1950s. Even the perception has changed. Martin Marty, in the June 15, 1995 edition of *Context: A Commentary on the Interaction of Religion and Culture* (vol. 27, no. 14), noted that at a recent Senate Finance Committee meeting, senators were struggling with how to characterize our national religious ethos. At one point Senator Moynihan commented, "It's now official. Ours is a *Judeo-Christian-Islamic* heritage. If anybody feels left out, we've got some more hyphens" (p. 1). It is in fact not easy to describe the religious ethos of the nation.

2. Diana L. Eck, "Neighboring," *Harvard Magazine* (September–October 1996), p. 40.

3. As we discussed in the doctoral seminar at Vanderbilt, the acknowledgment of diversity in key institutions varies according to the part of the country in which one lives. Laurel Cassidy, a student in the seminar, had worked in Nashville hospitals, where examples of cultural and religious diversity continued to be seen as exceptions for which no general policies were necessary. Laurel's paper sought to develop case studies of actual examples which could be used with health professionals to help alert them to the ways in which cultural and religious difference could affect their relations with patients.

4. Eck, "Neighboring," p. 44.

5. I want to thank Denis Thalson for pushing me beyond the much-invoked but less than specific notion of "common ground" to specify more clearly the challenge facing us.

6. Cornel West, *Race Matters* (New York: Vintage Books, 1994), p. 109.

7. After Vatican II, this situation changed dramatically, and Dubuque became a

leading center of ecumenical dialogue and cooperation. By the time of Vatican II, however, I was away at college. The Dubuque I knew was pre-Vatican II, a time when Catholics and Protestants perpetuated the religious competition which had long marked the community.

8. In college I had developed a profound interest in Greek mythology and its resonances through Western literature. Having discovered the richness of cultural allusion woven through Western art and literature, I developed a notion of what it was "to be educated"—I would be a person who could appreciate these allusions! The Chinese course brought home dramatically that there were voices and images of which I had not dreamed. This discovery paralleled the resurgence of many voices (women, nonelite, ethnic, dissenters, gays, and lesbians) which have challenged our notion of canon. The course on China was simply the gate through which I happened upon this discovery, but because of the enormous depth and richness of the Chinese literary and artistic heritage, the challenge to my previous notion of "culture" was resounding.

9. Carter Heyward, *Our Passion for Justice: Images of Power, Sexuality, and Liberation* (New York: Pilgrim Press, 1984), p. 245.

10. William E. Soothill, *Three Religions of China: Lectures Delivered at Oxford* (London: Oxford University Press, H. Milford, 1923), p. 13.

11. Valerie Hansen, *Changing Gods in Medieval China, 1127-1276* (Princeton: Princeton University Press, 1990), p. 3.

2. The Pilgrimage and the Pilgrim

1. Denis Thalson has reminded me that "a pilgrimage" is marked by the intention—generally religious—of the pilgrim. This is an important point. However, pilgrimages can creep up on you, so to speak, especially in East Asia. Scattered throughout China and Japan are famous historic pilgrimage routes. These routes are followed by groups of devout and committed pilgrims, true pilgrims in Denis's sense, in that they undertake their journey with a religious intent. However, the routes are also followed by tourists and visitors like Cynthia and myself, who may not have, or may not be aware of, the religious intent and shape of the journey. However, some, like myself, are taken by surprise (and grace) when the journey does in fact turn out to have a deeper meaning, and their motivations turn out to be deeper than they knew. As is also made clear in Wu Ch'eng-en's great novel of Chinese pilgrimage, *Journey to the West*, even committed pilgrims are likely to discover levels of meanings and intentions of the pilgrimage which are quite distinct from those they began with. As they travel, their understanding and insights grow.

2. This was an example of patriotism or national pride, since the Republic of Taiwan was proud of its membership in the United Nations and its permanent seat on the Security Council representing "China." However, close to the time of this pilgrimage, the U.N. voted to replace Taiwan with the People's Republic of China as the representative of China. That vote was traumatic for the Taiwan government. Since I have not returned to Shih T'ou Shan, I have not been able to determine whether this carousel remains. I suspect that it was removed in the period after the U.N. vote.

3. The Eight Immortals were colorful characters each reputed to offer a distinctive boon, such as long life, many sons, success in business, to devotees. They

represent the most pragmatic and this-worldly version of the Chinese religious imagination: religion offers specific blessings to enhance one's lot in this life. See Kwok Man Ho and Joanne O'Brien, trans. and ed., *The Eight Immortals of Taoism: Legends and Fables of Popular Taoism* (New York: Meridian, 1987).

It has long been a practice of scholars, both Chinese and Western, to label most religious practices or ideas under one of the so-called Three Teachings: Confucianism, Buddhism, and Taoism. The writings of anthropologists have added a fourth or "folk" label, recognizing that many practices cannot be included under the other three. As we will discuss in chapter 4, scholarship has increasingly questioned the boundaries between the Three Teachings and the accuracy of the labels. However, for the sake of clarity, I am sometimes compelled to use the labels. The use of quotation marks in this sentence indicates that although the Eight Immortals were conventionally labeled Taoist, they can equally be seen in the province of the amorphous folk traditions of China.

4. See Wolfram Eberhard, *The Local Cultures of South and East China* (Leiden: E.J. Brill, 1968).

5. It is a basic principle of Buddhist pedagogy that each seeker must learn for him- or herself. The skillful Buddhist teacher seeks to expose seekers to experiences or stories which will help them to find the truth, but does not offer truth on a platter.

6. I was fortunate to do a tutorial with William Theodore de Bary on Taoism and folk religions which greatly extended the boundaries of Columbia's core courses. This tutorial gave me a context of knowledge in which to place my observations of religious life.

7. In the *I Ching* (Book of Changes), the phrase "to cross the great waters" signifies an undertaking of significance and challenge.

8. See Barbara Aria with Russell Eng Gon, *The Spirit of the Chinese Character: Gifts from the Heart* (San Francisco: Chronicle Books, 1992), p. 19.

9. D. C. Lau, trans., *Lao Tzu, Tao te ching* (Middlesex, Eng.: Penguin Books, 1963), XXV, p. 82.

10. The Chinese divide the soul into an earthly and a heavenly component. The earthly component resides in the body, and—after death—in the grave until it is reabsorbed into the earth from which it came. The heavenly or spiritual portion carries the intellectual and spiritual powers of the human being; it is this spirit (*shen*) which travels to other realms and which hears the prayers of the filial descendants.

11. See, for instance, Yü Ying-shih, "'O Soul, Come Back!' A Study in Changing Conceptions of the Soul and Afterlife in Pre-Buddhist China," *Harvard Journal of Asiatic Studies* 47: 2 (Dec 84): 391; and C. Stevan Harrell, "The Concept of Soul in Chinese Folk Religion," *Journal of the Association of Asian Studies* 38:1 (May 79): 519-528. I thank Kevin Cheng for suggesting these references.

12. See Lu Kuan Yu, *Taoist Yoga, Alchemy and Immortality* (New York: Samuel Weiser, Inc., 1973), esp. xii-xvii and p. 68.

13. See Amy Tan, *Joy Luck Club* (New York: Putnam's, 1989), p. 240. Traditional Chinese society did not distinguish between fainting, coma, and death. It was just that some deaths became permanent. They were all "deaths" because the soul had left the body.

14. Many readers may have seen in museums versions of the Han ceramic models of horses, food, servants, and even barns and homes meant to supply the dead with the accoutrements of the living.

15. Different schools or lineages of Taoism developed and specialized in specific

rituals which teachers handed on to worthy disciples. Thunder rituals represented one of the many streams of Taoist rites. See Judith M. Boltz, *A Survey of Taoist Literature: Tenth to Seventeenth Centuries*, Chinese Research Monograph Series, no. 32 (Berkeley: Institute of East Asian Studies, 1987), pp. 47-49, 69-70, 176-179, and 263 n. 54.

16. The use of "Taoistic" in this case indicates that although *fang-wai* has been primarily associated with Taoism, it is a general pattern of Chinese religious life, and should not be considered Taoist in any clear sense.

17. Miyakawa Hisayuki, "Nansô no Dôshi Haku Gyozen no jiseki" (On the life of Southern Sung Taoist Master Pai Yü-ch'an), in *Uchida Gimpu hakushi shôju kinen tôyôshi ronshû* (A festschrift commemorating the sixtieth birthday of Professor Uchida Gimpu) (Kyoto: Dôhôsha, 1978), p. 502.

18. Miyakawa has documented examples of correspondence with members of the middle-level officialdom, notably Li Ch'en (1144-1218) and Ch'iao Li-hsien (1155-1222) (Miyakawa, "On the Life of Pai Yü-ch'an," 512), and there are a few disciples who have left some writings. My attempts to identify upwards of eighty persons named in poems and occasional writings proved fruitless. Pai's activities were primarily local and mostly among the subelite, although his contacts with abbots on Lung-hu shan and at Hsi-shan are reasonably well documented.

19. See Judith A. Berling, *The Syncretic Religion of Lin Chao-en* (New York: Columbia University Press, 1980), chapter 4.

20. See ibid., chapters 6 and 7.

21. Wu Ch'eng-en, *Journey to the West*, 4 vols., trans. Anthony Yü (Chicago: University of Chicago Press, 1977-1981).

22. See Christian Jochim, *Chinese Religions: A Cultural Perspective* (New Jersey: Prentice Hall, 1986), p. 106, for an explanation of the names.

23. *Journey to the West*, vol. 4, p. 391. In Buddhist teaching, all reality is "empty" of permanent existence; the wordless scriptures perfectly represent "reality as it is."

24. Chinese call foreigners *wai-kuo-jen*, literally, people of outside countries.

3. Forging a New Path

1. Ruben L. F. Habito, *Total Liberation: Zen Spirituality and the Social Dimension* (Maryknoll, NY: Orbis Books, 1989). See also Alan W. Watts, *The Art of Contemplation: A Facsimile Manuscript with Doodles by Alan Watts* (New York: Pantheon, 1972), and *The Spirit of Zen: A Way of Life, Work, and Art in the Far East* (New York: Grove Press, 1960); Thomas Merton, *Mystics and Zen Masters* (New York: Strauss and Giroux, 1967), and *Zen and the Birds of Appetite* (New York: New Directions, 1968).

2. John B. Cobb, *Beyond Dialogue: Toward a Mutual Transformation of Christianity and Buddhism* (Philadelphia: Fortress Press, 1982); Abe Masao, *Zen and Western Thought*, ed. William R. LaFleur (Honolulu: University of Hawaii Press, 1985).

3. Robert C. Neville, *The Tao and the Daimon: Segments of a Religious Inquiry* (Albany: State University of New York Press, 1982); Thomas P. Kasulis, *Self and Body in Asian Theory and Practice*, ed. Thomas P. Kasulis, with Roger T. Ames and Wimal Dissanayake (Albany: State University of New York Press, 1993).

4. Alan Race, *Christians and Religious Pluralism: Patterns in the Christian Theology of Religions* (London: SMC Press, 1982); John Hick and Paul F. Knitter,

eds., *The Myth of Christian Uniqueness: Toward a Pluralistic Theology of Religions* (Maryknoll, NY: Orbis Books, 1988); Francis X. Clooney, S.J., *Seeing through Texts: Doing Theology among Srivaisnavas of South India* (Albany: State University of New York Press, 1996).

5. See Jaroslav Pelikan, *The Christian Tradition: A History of the Development of Doctrine*, vol. 1, *The Emergence of the Catholic Tradition (100-600)* (Chicago: University of Chicago Press, 1971), esp. chapter 2, "Outside the Mainstream," pp. 67-120.

6. John Hick, "The Non-Absoluteness of Christianity," in *The Myth of Christian Uniqueness*, p. 17.

7. See Mark Heim, "Mapping Globalization for Theological Education," *Theological Education* 26, Supplement 1 (Spring, 1990): 9-10.

8. Traditionally, Christians have used the term "ecumenism" primarily to refer to their relations with other Christian groups and—in some cases—with the Jewish communities. However, the term *oecumene* refers to the "house," and has been historically used to refer to the whole world. Thus the term "wider ecumenism" has been coined as a way of extending the ecumenical attitude toward interfaith relations. See Peter Phan, "Introduction," in *Christianity and the Wider Ecumenism*, ed. Peter Phan (New York: Paragon House, 1990), pp. ix-x.

9. Alan Race, *Christians and Religious Pluralism*, chapter 2, pp. 10-37.

10. See, for example, his volume *Problems of Religious Pluralism* (New York: St. Martin's Press, 1985).

11. John Hick, "Rethinking Christian Doctrine in the Light of Religious Pluralism," in *Christianity and the Wider Ecumenism*, pp. 89-102.

12. This bears a striking resemblance to the much-criticized assimilationist approach to U.S. culture, which assumes that in the "melting pot," cultural differences could be melted away until groups became "American." What this means, in actuality, is that the cultural minorities are expected to conform to the mores and sensibilities of groups which had assumed the role of "mainstream cultural elite."

13. (Maryknoll, NY: Orbis Books, 1988).

14. (New York: Paragon House, 1990).

15. Langdon Gilkey, "Plurality and Its Theological Implications," in *The Myth of Christian Uniqueness*, p. 39.

16. Stanley J. Samartha, "The Cross and the Rainbow," in *The Myth of Christian Uniqueness*, p. 69.

17. Durwood Foster, "Christian Motives for Interfaith Dialogue," *Christianity and the Wider Ecumenism*, p. 24.

18. Ibid.; and Martin Forward, "How Do you Read?: The Scriptures in Interfaith Dialogue," in *Christianity and the Wider Ecumenism*, pp. 103-115.

19. Monika Hellwig, "The Wider Ecumenism: Some Theological Questions," in *Christianity and the Wider Ecumenism*, pp. 75-88; and M. Darrol Bryant, "Interfaith Encounter and Dialogue in a Trinitarian Perspective," in *Christianity and the Wider Ecumenism*, pp. 3-20.

20. Mary Ann Stenger, "The Understanding of Christ as Final Revelation," in *Christianity and the Wider Ecumenism*, pp. 191-206; Donald W. Dayton, "Karl Barth and the Wider Ecumenism," in *Christianity and the Wider Ecumenism*, pp. 181-190; and Frederick M. Jelly, "Tillich, Rahner, and Schillebeeckx on the Uniqueness and Universality of Christianity in Dialogue with the World Religions," in *Christianity and the Wider Ecumenism*, pp. 207-220.

21. Seiichi Yagi, "'I' in the Words of Jesus," in *The Myth of Christian Uniqueness*, pp. 117-134.

22. Myrtle S. Langley, "One More Step in a Journey of Many Miles: Toward a Theology of Interfaith Dialogue: Report, Reception, and Response," in *Christianity and the Wider Ecumenism*, pp. 221-232; Joseph Osei-Bonsu, "'Extra Ecclesiam nulla Salus': Critical Reflections from Biblical and African Perspectives," in *Christianity and the Wider Ecumenism*, pp. 131-146; Joseph H. Fichter, "Christianity as a World Minority,"in *Christianity and the Wider Ecumenism*, pp. 59-74.

23. Paul F. Knitter, "Toward a Liberation Theology," in *The Myth of Christian Uniqueness*, pp. 178-200; Rosemary Radford Ruether, "Feminism and Jewish-Christian Dialogue: Particularism and Universalism in the Search for Religious Truth," in *The Myth of Christian Uniqueness*, pp. 137-148; Marjorie Hewitt Suchocki, "Religious Pluralism from a Feminist Perspective," in *The Myth of Christian Uniqueness*, pp. 149-161.

24. Peter C. Phan, "Are There Other 'Saviors' for Other Peoples?: A Discussion of the Problem of the Universal Significance and Uniqueness of Jesus Christ," in *Christianity and the Wider Ecumenism*, p. 168.

25. John Hick, *God Has Many Names: Britain's New Religious Pluralism* (London: Macmillan, 1980), pp. 59-79.

26. Mary Ann Stenger, "The Understanding of Christ," p. 192.

27. Paul F. Knitter, "Toward a Liberation Theology."

28. S. Mark Heim, *Salvations: Truth and Difference in Religion* (Maryknoll, NY: Orbis Books, 1995), p. 187.

29. Ibid., p. 189.

30. Francis X. Clooney, *Seeing through Texts*, pp. 296-297.

31. Ibid., pp. 299-304.

32. From "Anything We Love Can Be Saved," an address by Alice Walker at the First Annual Zora Neale Hurston Festival, Eatonville, FL, January 26, 1990, cited in Playbill for "Spunk: Three Tales by Zora Neale Hurston," Berkeley Repertory Theater, November 1-December 21, 1991.

33. Anne C. Riessner, "Piece by Piece: A Mosaic of Global Theological Education," *Theological Education* 27.2 (Spring 1991): 113.

34. "Christian Motives," pp. 21-34.

35. This was one of the central insights in the theory of religions developed by Mircea Eliade, articulated in his classic, *The Sacred and the Profane: The Nature of Religion: The Significance of Religious Myth, Symbolism, and Ritual within Life and Culture* (New York: Harcourt, Brace, and World, 1959).

36. (Boston: Beacon Press, 1993).

37. In the Vanderbilt doctoral seminar, Emily Askew pointed out that my approach is pragmatic, offering a back, or at least a side door to avoid the obstacles of a more direct, head-on approach to the matter. This statement illumines how very Chinese my approach is. First, the Chinese are well-known for being profound religious pragmatists; they follow "what works" and what shows evidence of success. Second, Chinese architecture and *feng-shui* (geomancy, or the art arranging space so as to augment auspicious energies and to guard against negative forces) always argue against a straight pathway into the front door. Such a path, they believe, invites evil—human or otherwise. An obstacle needs to be erected to create bends or turns in the path, so that one goes around the side rather than entering directly.

38. Students in the Vanderbilt doctoral seminar, notably Laurel Cassidy, remind-ed me that there are limits to the mutual accessibility of symbols, and some are less transferable than others. The cross, for instance, is so profoundly embedded in the full Christian story that it would not appear to be easily accessible to non-Christians. My point is not the absolute, but the relative accessibility of symbols, which allow us to glimpse the views of another faith.

39. For another book starting from the premise that practice is a promising ground for interfaith understanding, see Robert Aitken and David Stendl-Rast, *The Ground We Share: Everyday Practice, Buddhist and Christian* (Boston: Shambhala, 1996), a dialogue between a Zen master and a Benedictine monk on issues of reli-gious practice.

40. By European and North American standards, Protestants and Catholics are both Christians, but in Asia these are viewed as two different religions. Even in Europe and North America, and despite post-Vatican II developments, there is a considerable historical and traditional gap between the traditions from which Protestants and Catholics have tended to draw.

41. Peter Feldmeier of the GTU wrote his doctoral dissertation on the issue of on what grounds would a Christian be able to practice Buddhist Vipassina medita-tion? What was at stake in such an inter-religious form of practice? See "Inter-relatedness: A Comparison of the Spiritualities of St. John of the Cross and Budhhaghosa for the Purpose of Examining the Christian Use of Buddhist Practices" (Doctoral dissertation, Graduate Theological Union, 1996).

4. Diversity and Competition in the Chinese Religious Field

1. The use of the term "religion" in regard to China is complex. There is no exact equivalent of the Western notion of religion (based on a Christian model) in classical Chinese. Tao (the Way) may be the closest equivalent. The Chinese used *chiao* (teaching) to refer to and classify philosophical, doctrinal, and spiritual ideas, writings, and practices. Sometimes, particularly in relation to Taoism, *tao-chiao* referred to religious practices and traditions, and *tao-chia* to philosophical thinkers.

Confucianism was deemed by early Christian missionaries, and thence by the Chinese themselves, not to be a religion in the Western sense. It does indeed lack certain characteristics of Western monotheistic religions (ordained clergy, rituals of membership, theistic beliefs). It was deemed a way of life or a sociomoral philoso-phy. Yet in the last thirty years, students of Chinese thought and religion have noted that Confucian beliefs, values, and observances are at the very heart of Chinese spir-itual life, and they intersect in complex ways with the more overtly "religious" prac-tices and beliefs of Taoism, Buddhism, and folk traditions. (See for instance Rodney L. Taylor's *The Religious Dimensions of Confucianism* [Albany: State University of New York Press, 1990].) Thus whether or not Confucianism is a religion depends on one's definition of "religion." Yet it is not possible to fully understand the dynamics of the Chinese religious world without taking Confucianism into account. (This was brilliantly illustrated in C. K. Yang's classic *Religion in Chinese Society: A Study of Contemporary Social Functions of Religion and Some of Their Historical Factors* [Berkeley: University of California Press, 1967].)

Given all this, while I acknowledge that "Confucianism" stretches one's defini-tion of religion and that most Chinese people would not call it a religion, I nonetheless treat it as part of the Chinese religious field and maintain that the practices and values of Confucianism have profound religious implications.

2. Jan Jakob Maria de Groot has catalogued these sectarian and divisive elements in his rather polemical tract, *Sectarianism and Religious Persecution in the History of Chinese Religions* (Amsterdam: J. Muller, 1903-4). See also C. K. Yang, "Confucian Thought and Chinese Religion," in *Chinese Thought and Institutions*, ed. John K. Fairbank (Chicago: University of Chicago Press, 1957), pp. 587-588.

3. In 1983, 120 million Japanese citizens recorded 220 million religious affiliations. See Josef Kreiner, "Religion in Japan," in *Japan*, ed. Manfred Pohl (Stuttgart, 1986), pp. 387-392. This reference is cited from Hans Küng, "Dual Religious Citizenship: A Challenge to the West," in Hans Küng and Julia Ching, *Christianity and Chinese Religions* (New York: Doubleday, 1989), p. 274.

4. On the *Thirteen Classics* and the *Four Books*, see *Sources of Chinese Tradition*, compiled by William Theodore de Bary, Wing-tsit Chan, Burton Watson (New York: Columbia University Press, 1964) I: 1-5 and 113.

5. Ibid., I: 239-250.

6. One of the best and most accurate surveys of Taoist lineages and literatures is Judith M. Boltz, *A Survey of Taoist Literature: Tenth to Seventeenth Centuries*, China Research Monograph No. 32 (Berkeley: Institute of East Asian Studies, 1987).

7. A somewhat dated but still usable survey of the arts of nurturing life is found in Holmes Welch, *The Parting of the Way* (Boston: Beacon Press, 1966), pp. 97-112, and 130-141.

8. For a classic introduction to Chinese Buddhism, see Kenneth K. S. Ch'en, *Buddhism in China: A Historical Survey* (Princeton: Princeton University Press, 1964).

9. In the last decade scholars of Chinese religion have begun major work on tracing the reconfiguration of lineages. See, for instance, Judith Magee Boltz, "Taoist Literature: Five Dynasties to Ming," in William Nienhauser, Jr., ed., *The Indiana Companion to Traditional Chinese Literature* (Bloomington: Indiana University Press, 1986), pp. 153 ff.; and Judith M. Boltz, *A Survey of Taoist Literature*.

10. C. K. Yang, *Religion in Chinese Society*, p. 25.

11. Robert Redfield suggested dealing with this problem by referring to Confucianism, Buddhism, and Taoism as the "great traditions" of China, and to the folk religions as the "little tradition." See his *Peasant Society and Culture: An Anthropological Approach to Civilization* (Chicago: University of Chicago Press, 1956), pp. 67-104. Such an approach, however, fails to do justice to the "folk" or popular elements of "great" traditions, and to elite patronage of "folk" traditions. Christian Jochim addresses the issue by discussing the religions of China under the title "The Four Traditions." See his *Chinese Religions: A Cultural Perspective* (New Jersey: Prentice Hall, 1986), esp. pp. 12-16. His approach is preferable to Redfield's, but may suggest a coherence which folk traditions simply do not sustain. I am grateful to Kevin Cheng for pressing me to clarify this point.

12. *Mencius* 3A:3; translated in *Sources of Chinese Tradition*, I: 95.

13. Gazetteers recorded information about local shrines and temples as well as local customs to record the distinctive religious practices of the region.

14. Stanley J. Tambiah, *Buddhism and Spirit Cults in North-east Thailand* (Cambridge: Cambridge University Press, 1970), chapter 19, pp. 337-350.

15. I thank the students in the Vanderbilt seminar for this image, which helps to escape the notion of a football or soccer field where teams defend opposing goals.

The latter clearly does not work in China. The point of the Chinese game is not to vanquish an opponent, but to gain maximum treasure (religious boon or fulfillment).

16. Pierre Bourdieu, "Genèse et structure du champ religieux" (Origin and structure of the religious field) *Revue Francaise de Sociologie* 12 (1971): 295-334.

17. The computer model suggested above would help here; once you plug in the group which is depicting the religious fields, all of the temples and paths would rearrange themselves accordingly.

18. See Kenneth K. S. Ch'en, *The Chinese Transformation of Buddhism* (Princeton, NJ: Princeton University Press, 1973), pp. 46-53, and *Shih shuo hsin yü: A New Account of Tales of the World* by Liu I-ch'ing with commentary by Liu Chün, trans. with introduction and notes by Richard B. Mather (Minneapolis: University of Minnesota Press, 1976).

19. Introduction to Mou Tzu, *Li-huo lun* "The Disposition of Error," in *Sources of Chinese Tradition* I: 274.

20. Chinese fears are articulated in ibid., in which he attacks Buddhism on the grounds that: 1) it is not mentioned in the Chinese classics; 2) monks are unfilial in that they harm their bodies and do not marry; and 3) Chinese should not be influenced by the ways of barbarians.

21. From *Fan-wang ching, Taishô tripitika* 24.10006a, 1007b; cited from Kenneth K. S. Ch'en, *Transformation of Chinese Buddhism*, p. 34.

22. *Erh-shih-ssu-hsiao ya-tso-wen* (British museum, Stein 3728, P I), cited from Kenneth K. Ch'en, *Transformation of Chinese Buddhism*, pp. 35-36.

23. Han Yü, "Memorial on the Bone of the Buddha," from *Ch'ang-li hsien-sheng wen-chi* (Collected Writings of Master Han Yü), in *Sources of Chinese Tradition*, I: 373-374.

24. Kenneth K. Ch'en, *Transformation of Chinese Buddhism*, pp. 125-178.

25. From *Chiu T'ang-shu* (Older T'ang History), in *Sources of Chinese Tradition*, I: 380-381.

5. Cultural Unity and Local Variation

1. The term "myth" is used here not in the colloquial sense of something which is not true, but in the religious sense of a story which seeks to define a community's sense of reality in such a way as to ground it in a central ideal. As we shall see, the Chinese had as much trouble living up to their myths or ideals as any people, but the myths nonetheless had formative and defining power.

2. See David N. Keightley, "The Religious Commitment: Shang Theology and the Genesis of Chinese Political Culture," *History of Religions* 17:3,4 (Feb-May, 1978): 211-225.

3. Cosmology is the science of the cosmos, beliefs about the entire order of being. A cosmological system, then, is a view about the order and structure of all that is.

4. Tung Chung-shu, *Ch'un-ch'iu fan-lu*, Sec. 43, 11:5a-b; in William Theodore de Bary, Wing-tsit Chan, Burton Watson, *Sources of Chinese Tradition* (New York: Columbia University Press, 1960), vol. 1, pp. 163-164.

5. See Kenneth Scott Latourette, *The Chinese: Their History and Culture*, 4th ed. (New York: Macmillan, 1964), pp. 78-87; and Wolfram Eberhard, *A History of China*, 4th ed. (Berkeley: University of California Press, 1987), pp. 47-59.

6. Valerie Hansen, for instance, has studied the government practice of granting titles to gods in a symbolic effort to express the emperor's patronage of and control over the divine realm. See *Changing Gods in Medieval China, 1127-1276* (Princeton: Princeton University Press, 1990), pp. 79-104.

7. See, for instance, Chün-fang Yü, *The Renewal of Buddhism in China: Chu-hung and the Late Ming Synthesis* (New York: Columbia University Press, 1981), pp. 144-170; and Arthur F. Wright, "T'ang T'ai-tsung and Buddhism," in *Perspectives on the T'ang*, ed. Arthur F. Wright and Denis Twitchett (New Haven: Yale University Press, 1973), pp. 261-263.

8. Local gazetteers, by contrast, contained sections on "local customs" and "shrines and temples" which recorded these traditions in some specificity.

9. See William Theodore de Bary, "Chinese Despotism and the Confucian Ideal: A Seventeenth-Century View" (pp. 178-180) and E.A. Kracke, Jr., "Region, Family, and Individual in the Chinese Examination System" (pp. 251-268), in John K. Fairbank, ed., *Chinese Thought and Institutions* (Chicago: University of Chicago Press, 1957).

10. Jan Jakob Maria de Groot, *Sectarianism and Religious Persecution in the History of Chinese Religions* (Amsterdam: J. Muller, 1903-1904); T'ao Hsi-sheng, *Ming-tai tsung-chiao* (Ming dynasty religion) (Taipei: Tai-wan hsüeh-sheng shu-chü, 1968); Mano Senryû, *Mindai bunkashi kenkyû* (The cultural history of the Ming dynasty) (Kyoto: Dôhôsha, 1979).

11. The Ch'ang-sheng chiao of the eighteenth century is a case in point. See Daniel L. Overmyer, *Folk Buddhist Religion: Dissenting Sects in Late Traditional China* (Cambridge, MA: Harvard University Press, 1976), pp. 7-11. See also, Susan Naquin, *Millenarian Rebellion in China: The Eight Trigrams Uprising of 1813* (New Haven: Yale University Press, 1976) and *Shantung Rebellion: The Wang Lun Uprising of 1774* (New Haven: Yale University Press, 1981).

12. See David Johnson, "The City-God Cults of T'ang and Sung China," *Harvard Journal of Asiatic Studies* 45:2 (Dec 1985): 363-457; and Stephan Feuchtwang, "School-Temple and City God," in G. William Skinner, ed., *The City in Late Imperial China* (Stanford: Stanford University Press, 1977), pp. 581-608. The origins of Chinese local deities are not unlike the processes by which local saints come to be venerated within folk Catholicism.

13. The historical process of the development of the Chinese language was vastly more complex than this statement suggests. These examples are meant only to convey some of the distinctive characteristics of this nonalphabetic language system.

14. Alert readers will wonder how educated officials from various parts of the realm communicated with each other. They did so partly in writing, but they also developed a spoken language for the court (*kuan-hua*, lit. language of officials), which was a somewhat stilted and literary form of Peking dialect.

15. In late imperial China, some writers began experimenting with writing stories or fiction in language at least strongly colored by local dialect. The style was sometimes known as *pan-wen pan-pai* (half classical, half vernacular). As more authors sought to write in the vernacular language, local language and perceptions were more and more clearly reflected in literature. Only in the twentieth century did written vernacular fully develop, so that literature could be written in something like the spoken language. Once vernacular writing took hold, however, Peking dialect had to be promoted as a standard language, or else the plethora of dialects would have fragmented Chinese literature.

16. Victor H. Mair, "Language and Ideology in the Written Popularizations of the *Sacred Edict*," in David Johnson, Andrew Nathan, and Evelyn S. Rawski, eds., *Popular Culture in Late Imperial China* (Berkeley: University of California Press, 1985), pp. 325-359.

17. See, for example, Robert H. Hegel's analysis of *The Water Margin* in *The Novel in Seventeenth-Century China* (New York: Columbia University Press, 1981), pp. 67-84; and Paul S. Ropp, *Dissent in Early Modern China: Ju-lin wai-shih and Ch'ing Social Criticism* (Ann Arbor: University of Michigan Press, 1981).

18. Barbara E. Ward, "Varieties of the Conscious Model," in Michael P. Banton, ed., *The Relevance of Models for Social Anthropology* (London: Tavistock Publications, 1968), pp. 113-137.

19. The rituals associated with the early cult appear to have been "an early regional variation deeply rooted in the 'Taoist' Ling-pao heritage." See Judith M. Boltz, *A Survey of Taoist Literature: Tenth to Seventeenth Centuries*, China Research Monograph Series, Number 32 (Berkeley: Institute of East Asian Studies of the University of California, 1987), p. 71.

20. See Pai Yü-ch'an, "Ching-yang Hsü chen-chün chuan" (Biography of Realized Gentleman Hsü Ching-yang) in *Yü-lung chi* (Record of Yü-lung), ch. 33, preserved in *Hsiu-chen shih-shu*, in the *Tao-tsang*, Harvard Yenching #263.

21. Jurchen invaders from Central Asia, who ruled North China from 1115-1234. The remnant Sung government in the South was waging a battle to expel the invaders and to keep them from invading South China as well.

22. Note the similarity in reasoning to that behind the deity of the city-wall temple; his concern is to protect the local region, but this is presented as loyal aid to the throne.

23. The reader may be wondering why the emperor did not make the connection to Hsü Sun's divination system and the temple Sung emperors had previously patronized. The account does not explain, but it is noteworthy that deities could be known by several names or titles. For some reason (either faulty memory or an alternate name), the emperor did not make the connection and had to order a search for the temple.

24. The ritual document of the feast was preserved and published in Pai Yü-ch'an's life of Hsü Sun. "Ching-yang Hsü chen-chün."

25. "Ching-yang Hsü chen-chün chuan," 34.1a-5b.

26. The *chiao* was the highest ritual of organized Taoism, and could only be performed by Taoist priests with specialized training. See Michael R. Saso, *Taoism and the Rite of Cosmic Renewal* (Pullman: Washington State University Press, 1972), pp. 84-94.

27. "Ching-yang Hsü chen-chün chuan," 34.8b-10a.

6. Myriad Spirits and the Transcendent

1. I saw the same sort of authentic faith and spirituality in the Chinese worship of images that Diana Eck observed in the religious practices of Hindus in India. See Diana L. Eck, *Encountering God: A Spiritual Journey from Bozeman to Banaras* (Boston: Beacon, 1993). There are also striking similarities between Chinese veneration of their deities and popular Roman Catholic veneration of Our Lady of Guadalupe. These similarities merit scholarly study to advance our understanding of popular spiritualities.

2. Note the similarity between this and the animal carvings of native groups available for sale in the United States which, when prepared and blessed in the proper ritual environment, would become fetishes rather than mere carvings.

3. This belief in ritual vivification contrasts with Roman Catholic views of images, which are understood to be holy, but not inhabited by the saint.

4. Valerie Hansen, *Changing Gods in Medieval China 1127-1276* (Princeton: Princeton University Press, 1990), pp. 52-59.

5. A goddess who protects, among others, those who travel on water. Her main temple is in Fukien province in China, but she was very popular throughout southeast China and in Taiwan.

6. The example of the branch temple clearly illustrates that the deity is not fully or exclusively present in any one image; there may be thousands of such images around China. It also points out that each deity has a sacred site at which he or she is most effectively present. This main temple of a deity is the locus at which one can have fullest access to the spiritual power of the deity.

7. Laurence G. Thompson, *Chinese Religion: An Introduction*, 2d ed. (Encino, CA: Dickenson Publishing, 1975), p. 57.

8. *Chiang-su chin-shih*, 10:22a, cited in Hansen, *Changing Gods*, p. 24. There is a temporal gap of some eight hundred years between Hansen's examples and those from anthropological field observation. In juxtaposing these examples, I do not mean to ignore the fact that there were changes in the Chinese religious field over eight centuries. Nonetheless, the mutual illumination of these temporally distant sources testifies to powerful continuities in the basic dynamics of the Chinese religious field.

9. See Alvin P. Cohen, "Coercing the Rain Deities in Ancient China," *History of Religions* 17:3,4 (Feb-May, 1978): 244-265. See also Stephen Feuchtwang, "School-Temple and City God," in G. William Skinner, ed., *The City in Late Imperial China*, (Stanford: Stanford University Press, 1977), p. 603; and C. K. Yang, *Religion in Chinese Society: A Study of Contemporary Social Functions of Religion and Some of Their Historical Factors* (Berkeley and Los Angeles: University of California Press, 1967), p. 25.

10. Hansen, *Changing Gods*, p. 29.

11. Ibid., p. 47. Romanization system adapted for consistency with this text.

12. Ibid., p. 33. This is, roughly, the Chinese equivalent of "There are no atheists in fox holes."

13. Ibid., p. 34.

14. See *Reflections on Things at Hand: The Neo-Confucian Anthology Compiled by Chu Hsi and Lü Tsu-ch'ien*, trans. with notes by Wing-tsit Chan (New York: Columbia University Press, 1967), #33 (p. 26) and #46 (p. 32).

15. Arthur P. Wolf, "Gods, Ghosts, and Ancestors," in Arthur P. Wolf, ed., *Religion and Ritual in Chinese Society* (Stanford: Stanford University Press, 1974), pp. 131-182.

16. Hansen, *Changing Gods*, p. 9.

17. This is a major motif, for instance, in Wu Ch'eng-en's famous *Hsi-yu chi* (Journey to the West). The three guardians were promoted or (more frequently) demoted in the heavenly ranks because of their good or bad deeds; having slipped badly, they are assigned to guard Tripitika to expiate their faults and begin to regain their standing in the heavenly ranks.

18. C. Stevan Harrell, "When a Ghost Becomes a God," in *Religion and Ritual in Chinese Society*, pp. 193-206.

19. The term "posit" here reflects the fact that the human conceptualization of Tao or the ultimate source was required in part by the multiplicity. The Tao or source pre-exists and transcends human conceptualization, but the Chinese are quite clear about the distinction between their conceptualizations and the Tao in itself.

20. *Lao Tzu, Tao te ching*, trans. D. C. Lau (Middlesex: Penguin, 1963), I, p. 57.

21. *Chuang Tzu*, chapt. 22; in *The Complete Works of Chuang Tzu*, trans. Burton Watson (New York: Columbia University Press, 1968), p. 241.

22. Hansen, *Changing Gods*, p. 36. Romanization of Kuan-yin adapted to be consistent with this book's style.

23. Based on the field observation and scholarly analysis of Michael R. Saso in *Taoism and the Rite of Cosmic Renewal* (Pullman: Washington State University Press, 1972).

24. Ibid., p. 32.

25. Ibid., pp. 43-44.

26. Valerie Hansen notes that because of the sale of ordination certificates in the Sung dynasty (as opposed to the examination system for certifying ordination), there was considerable slippage in the training of priests for particular ceremonies, even the *chiao. Changing Gods*, p. 44.

27. See Michael R. Saso, *Taoism and the Rite of Cosmic Renewal*, pp. 38-41 and 51-52.

28. Ibid., chapters 2 and 4.

7. Many Embodiments of the Way

1. See Ainslee T. Embree, ed., *The Hindu Tradition* (New York: Modern Library, 1966), pp. 197-205.

2. These represent various names for the ultimate, the Sacred, in various Chinese religious streams.

3. See William Theodore de Bary, *The Liberal Tradition in China* (New York: Columbia University Press, 1982), pp. 32-37; Monika Ubelhor, "The Community Compact (Hsiang-yüeh) of the Sung and its Educational Significance," in William Theodore de Bary and John W. Chaffee, eds., *Neo-Confucian Education: The Formative Stage* (Berkeley: University of California Press, 1989), pp. 371-388; Chu Hsi, *Tseng-sun Lü-shih hsiang-yüeh* (Amended community compact of Mr. Lü), in *Chu tzu ta-ch'üan* (The great compendium of writings of Master Chu) (Ssu-pu pei-yao ed.) 74: 23a-29b. I thank Kevin Cheng for his assistance in developing this note.

4. See Judith Berling, "Bringing the Buddha Down to Earth: Notes on the Emergence of Yü-lu as a Buddhist Genre," *History of Religions* 27: 1 (August, 1987): 56-88.

5. Preface by Chu Hsi to *Chin-ssu lu*, in *Reflections on Things at Hand: The Neo-Confucian Anthology Compiled by Chu Hsi and Lü Tsu-ch'ien*, trans. and with notes by Wing-tsit Chan (New York: Columbia University Press, 1967), p. 2. The exclusive language may be grating to the modern reader, but in this case the kind of study indicated in the statement would have been open only to males. Yet the principle about the *intent* of the book would be applicable, in a contemporary setting, to Confucians of both genders.

6. See Berling, "Bringing the Buddha Down to Earth."

7. Preface to *Chu-tzu yü-lei* (Categorized sayings of Master Chu), ed. Li Ching-te (reprinted, Taipei: Cheng-chung shu- chü, 1962), 1: 1.

8. Analects of Confucius 1: 6; cited from *Sources of Chinese Tradition*, compiled by William Theodore de Bary, Wing-tsit-Chen, Burton Watson (New York: Columbia University Press, 1964), 1: 24. Translation adapted for inclusive language.

9. Wang Yang-ming, *Ch'uan-hsi lu* (Instructions for Practical Living), in *A Source Book for Chinese Philosophy*, trans. and comp. by Wing-tsit Chan (Princeton: Princeton University Press, 1963), p. 669; see also pp. 10-11.

10. Preface to *Chin-ssu lu*, cited in Chan, *Reflections*, p. 2.

11. There is a large literature on the differences between oral and literate cultures, and the impact of writing and books, and also an emerging literature on the different *concepts and uses* of books and writing in various cultures. Although writing was venerated in China from a very early date, the importance of recitation maintained the oral aspects of learning and reinforced the link between learning and human behavior. The Chinese throughout their history lamented learning which became too bookish and abstract and failed to bear fruit in the living of human life.

12. Lin Chao-en, *Hsin-sheng chih-chih* (Direct pointing to the Mind as Sage) II: 2.3b, translated in Judith A. Berling, *The Syncretic Religion of Lin Chao-en* (New York: Columbia University Press, 1980), p. 131.

13. See *Neo-Confucian Education: The Formative Stage*, ed. William Theodore de Bary and John Chaffee (Berkeley: University of California Press, 1989); and Tadao Sakai, "Confucianism and Popular Educational Works," in *Self and Society in Ming Thought*, William Theodore de Bary and the Conference on Ming Thought (New York: Columbia University Press, 1970), pp. 331-366.

14. *Su Shih I-chuan* (Su Shih's comments on the Book of Changes), 9.190; in Kidder Smith, Jr., Peter K. Bol, Joseph A. Adler, Don J. Wyatt, eds., *Sung Dynasty Uses of the I Ching* (Princeton: Princeton University Press, 1990), p. 89.

15. Analects of Confucius, 4: 15, in *Sources*, 1: 25.

16. Ibid., 7: 8; in *Sources*, 1: 24. Translation adapted for inclusive language.

17. Ibid., 9: 10, in *Sources* 1: 25. Adapted for inclusive language.

18. Ibid., 7: 4; 7: 38; in *Sources* 1: 20.

19. Ibid., 7: 1; in *Sources* 1: 23.

20. Ibid., 4: 8; in *Sources*, 1: 23.

21. Ibid., 7: 25; *Sources* 1: 24.

22. *The Complete Works of Chuang Tzu*, trans. Burton Watson (New York: Columbia University Press, 1968), chapter 25, p. 281, 282-283. Translation adapted for inclusive language; this is particularly apt in the *Chuang Tzu* since several of the sages or teachers depicted in the book are women.

23. Ibid., chapter 19; pp. 205-206.

24. Lao Tzu, *Tao Te Ching*, chapt. 20. Translations combined from *Lao Tzu, Tao Te Ching*, trans. with an introduction by D. C. Lau (Middlesex, Eng.: Penguin, 1963), pp. 76-77; and Arthur Waley, *The Way and Its Power: A Study of Tao Te Ching and Its Place in Chinese Thought*, Arthur Waley (New York: Grove Press, 1958) pp. 168-169.

25. Lao Tzu, *Tao Te Ching*, D. C. Lau, trans., chapt. 17; p. 73.

8. Hospitality and the Chinese Religious Field

1. Arthur P. Wolf, "Gods, Ghosts, and Ancestors," in Arthur P. Wolf, ed., *Religion and Ritual in Chinese Society* (Stanford: Stanford University Press, 1974), pp. 131-182.

2. This applies even when the guest is of higher social status than the host, although it is true that in Chinese society the rituals of entertainment would vary according to the relative social positions of host and guest. I thank Kevin Cheng for this comment.

3. See C. K. Yang, *Religion in Chinese Society: A Study of Contemporary Social Functions of Religion and Some of Their Historical Factors* (Berkeley and Los Angeles: University of California Press, 1967), pp. 81-103.

4. This story was repeated often in the history of various religious groups in China, and was also a well-established pattern in the history of Buddhism going back to India. For instance, the four kings which guard the four corners of the Buddhist altar were vanquished and assimilated deities of Hindu and other local cults.

5. See Kristofer Schipper, "Neighborhood Cult Associations in Traditional Tainan," in G. William Skinner, ed., *The City in Late Imperial China* (Stanford: Stanford University Press, 1977), pp. 651-676.

6. See James Hayes, *The Hong Kong Region, 1850-1911: Institutions and Leadership in Town and Countryside* (Hamden, CT: Archon Books, 1977), pp. 98-101.

7. Jan Jakob Maria de Groot, in his multivolumed description of the practice of religion in southeast China at the turn of the century, described in wonderful detail the conspicuous display of Chinese weddings and funerals. Anthropological studies have reconfirmed his findings in a number of other sites. Jan Jakob Maria de Groot, *The Religious System of China: Its Ancient Forms, Evolution, History and Present Aspect, Manners, Customs, and Social Institutions Connected Therewith*, 7 Vols. (Amsterdam: J. Muller, c. 1901-04; reprinted by Ch'eng-wen Publishing Company, Taipei, 1969).

8. This contribution is roughly parallel to our custom that guests should bring a gift to a wedding or party.

9. Donald DeGlopper, "Religion and Ritual in Lukang," in *Religion and Ritual in Chinese Society*, p. 54.

10. A similar occurrence in eighteenth-century England was documented in Keith Thomas's classic *Religion and the Decline of Magic* (New York: Scribner and Sons, 1971), pp. 556-569.

11. Valerie Hansen discusses the sources through which the literate and illiterate heard about gods and miracles during the Sung dynasty in her introduction to *Changing Gods in Medieval China, 1127-1276* (Princeton: Princeton University Press, 1990), pp. 3-28.

12. For the code of offerings appropriate to deities of various classes, see Arthur Wolf, "Gods, Ghosts, and Ancestors," in *Religion and Ritual in Chinese Society*, pp. 131-182.

13. Emily Ahern has explored the intriguing parallels between petitioning deities and the government in her *Chinese Ritual and Politics* (Cambridge: Cambridge University Press, 1981), esp. pp. 2-24, 95-108.

14. When I visited two Buddhist monasteries in the People's Republic of China in October 1996, I noted that the restoration of wall paintings and carvings were

still serving this purpose. Visitors asked many questions about these illustrations in an effort to educate themselves about the Buddhist heritage.

15. See Chikusa Masaaki, *Chûkoku Bukkyô shakaishi kenkyû*(On the Social History of Chinese Buddhism) (Kyoto: Dôhôsha, 1982).

16. Such shops were doing a thriving business at Lion's Head Mountain. For the historical precedents, see G. William Skinner, *The City in Late Imperial China*, pp. 3-31, 211-252, 253-351.

17. See Holmes Welch, *The Practice of Chinese Buddhism, 1900-1950* (Cambridge, MA: Harvard University Press, 1967), pp. 303-356.

18. These are all recorded in the mountain gazetteer: *Wu-i shan-chih* (Mount Wu-i gazetteer), 24 ch., ed. Tung T'ien-kung (1846), Reprinted in *Chung-kuo ming-shan sheng-chi ts'ung-kan* (Compendium of the Scenic and Historic Traces of Famous Chinese Mountains).

19. One of the sadder legacies of the Cultural Revolution in China today is that the reconstruction of temple complexes has lost this multireligious dimension. Since Taoist sources are paying for Taoist restorations and Buddhist for Buddhist, the restored temple complexes are more religiously homogeneous than in the past; this development erodes the traditional Chinese religious field.

20. Michael Saso identifies the "red-head" priests as follows: "Members of this class are expected to cure sickness, win blessing, expel demons, and, in general, perform rituals for the living." Michael Saso, *Taoism and the Rite of Cosmic Renewal* (Pullman: Washington State University Press, 1972), p. 84. The red-head refers to a distinctive red scarf worn by such priests, not to red hair, which would be truly rare in Chinese society.

21. Since I also tried to record the music there are several quite hilarious tapes of funeral music accompanied by the under-beat of my feet running along the pavement. I pray that these not fall into other hands, giving rise to some theory of strange Chinese drumming traditions.

9. Christians and Religious Neighbors

1. The Buddhist term for pedagogical strategies geared to the level of understanding and spiritual maturity of one's audience.

2. I mean the term "theological" in the broadest possible sense, since my reflections focused primarily on religious behavior, practice, and pedagogy. I do not aspire to systematic theology.

3. Many participants in the dialogue have developed promising principles for Christian participation in such conversations (the most common one being that one cannot be an effective partner in conversation unless one brings one's beliefs and values with one), but these principles are not well known in the Christian communities.

4. See for example my book on syncretist Lin Chao-en, for whom such reconciliation was a major concern. Judith Berling, *The Syncretic Religion of Lin Chao-en* (New York: Columbia University Press, 1980).

5. My thank to James Keddy of Sacramento for informing me about the network.

6. I met this person at the National Interfaith Network in Wichita, Kansas, 1988.

7. Rosemarie Tong, *Feminist Thought: A Comprehensive Introduction* (Boulder,

CO: Westview Press, 1989), p. 7. Cited in Linda Moody, *Women Encounter God: Theology across Boundaries of Difference* (Maryknoll, NY: Orbis Books, 1996), p. 132.

8. Linda Moody, *Women Encounter God*, pp. 124-125.

9. This case is made by Karen Armstrong in *A History of God: The 4,000 Year Quest of Judaism, Christianity, and Islam* (New York: Ballantine Books, 1993).

10. *Hadewijch: The Complete Works*, trans. and intro. by Mother Columba Hart, O.S.B. (New York: Paulist Press, 1980), pp. 346-349.

11. Linda Moody, *Women Encounter God*, p. 111.

12. Thomas W. Ogletree, *Hospitality to the Stranger: Dimensions of Moral Understanding* (Philadelphia: Fortress Press, 1985), pp. 2-3.

13. Ibid., p. 3.

14. Ibid., p. 4.

15. Diana L. Eck, *Encountering God: A Spiritual Journey from Bozeman to Banaras* (Boston: Beacon Press, 1993), p. 79.

Index